THE

AFTE

REVIEW

Issue Three

SPRING
2026

AFTER TRAUMA THERE IS STILL POETRY

edited by

MAX WALLIS

contributing editors

DR ANNA PERCY
SUZI FEAY

ISSN: 2976-9752
ISBN: 978-1-0676046-2-2

Typeset by Max Wallis
Design by Max Wallis
Cover by Max Wallis
Edited by Max Wallis, Dr Anna Percy and Suzi Feay
Printed by 4edge Ltd
Published May 2026

We welcome submissions of poetry.
www.aftershockreview.com

On Form and the Poetic Field

At *The Aftershock Review*, we honour the integrity of each poet's chosen form. Some write entirely in lowercase, others adhere to sentence case, while some forgo conventional grammar and punctuation. These stylistic decisions are deliberate, reflecting the poet's voice, rhythm, and experience.

As a journal dedicated to exploring trauma, survival, and the complexities of lived experience, we do not impose a rigid house style. We recognise that form is a vital component of meaning. Whether through syntactical fragmentation, spatial dissonance, or the absence of conventional markers, a poem's structure is often inseparable from its emotional and thematic weight.

We preserve these choices as they appear in the poet's submission, ensuring that each piece is presented as intended—raw, precise, and unaltered in its expression of form. Of course, every poem has been carefully proofread and prepared for publication, respecting the poet's vision while ensuring clarity where needed.

In April 2025, *The Aftershock Review* received full funding from Arts Council England. In March 2026, it happened again.

In September 2025, *The Aftershock Review* received a one-off grant from the T. S. Eliot Foundation.

LOTTERY FUNDED
Supported using public funding by
ARTS COUNCIL ENGLAND

T. S. ELIOT FOUNDATION

ALSO AVAILABLE

THE AFTERSHOCK REVIEW

Issue One

Issue Two

POCKET AFTERSHOCKS

Psychosis and Our Other Madnesses

Dirty Laundry

CONTENTS

EDITORIAL NOTE BY MAX WALLIS

Issue One named the damage. Issue Two mapped the fragments that remain. Issue Three begins somewhere stranger, and perhaps more dangerous: with a question. *What do we need but a bit of hope?*

Not hope as cure, necessarily. Nor is it hope as slogan. It's not even the soft ribbon tied around suffering once the hard part is over. The poems gathered here know better than that. They know hope is often partial, awkward and badly lit. In Aaron Kent's "Night Repairs", it is a small screwdriver kept in a wallet for whatever the night needs fixing. In Hollie McNish's "in loving memory of the kissing tree", it is the tenderness of a first kiss, the hope of youth and innocence, setting the bar for all that follows. In Katie Hale's "What if we kissed inside the taxidermied Gothenburg blue whale?", hope becomes vast and strange: a love so big they have to tear down walls to let it in. Penny Sharman's "Pink Moon" offers a spell-like lunar interrogation, changing names as love, age, memory and bills circle. In Rosie Jackson's "Hymn to that Night", hope takes the form of praise: for the body, for survival, for the "trumpet that sounds". In Oliver James Lomax's poem, hope is a nonverbal child dancing while the poet holds a live baby chicken and the world, briefly, holds him upright.

In *An Anthropology of Grief*, the dead are not gone. They are handled, catalogued, emailed, scattered, preserved, misremembered, bought back from charity shops, carried in the throat. Catherine Redford invents rituals for the beloved dead: canopic jars, bees, wildflowers, AI portraits, feathers tucked into books left half-read. Gemma Strang turns post-mortem reports into unbearable intimacy: the exact weight of a parent's heart, the body rendered as data, grief forced to read the measurements. Sally Read's ashes refuse transcendence; they are flour-bags, cement dust, weather, a body returned as grit and residue. Clare Best honours the gaps left by a mother. Daragh Byrne stands inside the exact moment of a father's death. Stephen Boyce turns funeral and myth into "simple expressions of love". This is grief not as abstraction, but as matter.

Then the issue enters *The Rear Bedroom*. Abeer Ameer's poems insist on witness with forensic exactitude: the bed, the children, the Quran, the blood, the body, the wall, the number written on a child's cheek. There is no metaphor strong enough to replace the fact of what happened. Özge Lena extends this chamber of atrocity through bloodstones, war, beach, scar, cradle, missile, painting and Scheherazade-like survival. These poems are difficult because they are precise. They remind us that poetry must sometimes be evidence.

The Happiness Business understands family as something half-remembered and structurally unsound. These poems move through mothers, brothers, television light, classrooms, ambulances, inherited language and the strange labour of trying to reconstruct happiness from fragments. Adrian Slatcher's title gives the section its painful intelligence: happiness as something once known, then lost, then impossible to reconstruct "from the few clues we've got". Benedicta Norell writes the mother's words stuck like Hubba Bubba under a classroom desk. Dan O'Brien's Christmas Eve box becomes the "unwanted gift" of a brother's suicide.

Tom Branfoot's mother poems move through ambulance, divorce, smashed plates, breath, television blue and grief. Family here is not a theme. It alters the pressure system of every room it enters.

In *What Else Is a Body For?* the body appears scanned, medicated, judged, exhausted, side-effected, hungry, translated into data and returned again to tenderness. Elizabeth Eger's MRI turns the self into ribbon, mirage, coral reef and erased music. Hilary Hares holds failed hope, medication, judgement and grief in a chemist car park. Jessica Mookherjee asks when a body becomes "sub-optimum". Luke Samuel Yates turns side effects into a delirious street of odds, chips, mannequins and weather. Maura Dooley distils care into wire, tube, cord and "the many accents of love". Graham Mort stands beside stroke, snow, ward-light and hunger. The body keeps speaking, but it does not always explain itself.

Safety Checks is the issue's coldest section. Fiona Sampson wakes before waking into dumb shadow and invasive procedure. Xingyu Zhao's psych ward holds winter jacaranda, bento boxes, plastic spoons and a head of black hair beating beneath wings. Valentina Fulginiti repeats the language of protection until it becomes indictment: "some details have been altered to protect / the emotional safety of the offenders". Julie Stevens brings tigers into the wardrobe and A&E, where everyone has their own bites. Safety here is double-edged. It is being kept, watched, missed, mishandled, believed too late.

Five Years Is No Time at All meanwhile understands childhood as a present tense. Clementine Mendelson's poems are full of worms, compost, linoleum, locked doors, hospital corridors and all that still comes "crawling out". Hélène Demetriades turns a childhood newt, a father's blows, coneflowers, cousin, leak and house-damage into a single atmosphere of threat and memory. Stuart Charlesworth moves through swimming lessons, lizard transformations, complicity and rumours of tunnels beneath the village. Trish Reeves extends the sense that childhood is not what happened once. It is what the body keeps rehearsing.

In *Desire Inside a Yearning for the Deep*, desire becomes risk, scale, comedy, danger and transformation. Italo Ferrante writes queer terror through Carrie, cinema, shame, sex, prayer closets and the body under spectacle. Thomas Stewart gives us fallen angels, giants, sea-crowns and mythic longing. Yuri Leving's woman-knife unfolds tools, wounds, clocks and blades. Wanting here is never simple. It can bless, expose, cut, consume, remake.

On Not Speaking gathers the fractures of language, nation and inheritance. Maha Salih moves through Babylon, a stolen green-glazed brick, a father's defection and Arabic as both gift and loss. Raymond Antrobus stands in Dublin among protest, Englishness, silence and the limits of allegiance. These poems ask what happens when language is homeland, wound, border and failed rescue.

Within Ringroads is place as pressure. Alison Tanik's Ireland is full of swimming sheep, dead foxes, fossils, Famine houses, peat and rain. Katherine Horrex's ring roads hold beer-coloured trout, chipped mills, Chicken Cottage, tanning salons, doctored cars and regional grotesque. Steven Green's ceramic works bring propaganda, domestic object and political atmosphere into uneasy relation. These are not background landscapes. They are sites where history, class, absurdity and unease keep accumulating.

In *The Lake Into Which All Things Are Sunk*, Georgia Hilton gives us keys, CDs, fake IDs, brutality and guilty stones dropped into the lakebed. Alison Zhang's poems move through neurological slippage, buried mirrors, paper bodies, scissors, doors without handles and selves that do not quite stay put. This is a section of reflection and distortion, of evidence submerged but not erased.

The Image Has Failed Us turns to representation itself. Sue Hubbard's Auerbach poem searches for the edge between reality and essence, knowing that to become visible is also to become vulnerable. Suzi Feay writes voice, rest, intimacy and the difficulty of saying what can be carried for another person. Laura Theis places elegy inside screens, thresholds, yoga, disappearance and the unstable rituals of modern grief. Images, paintings, messages, bodies and portraits can hold something. They cannot hold enough.

Finally, *I'm Here, Love, the Cavalry Are on Their Way* brings the issue towards rescue, though never the simple kind. It leaves the issue suspended somewhere between rescue and exhaustion: the hope that someone might still arrive, even late, even carrying only language. The title itself carries the tenderness and absurdity of survival: the promise that someone is coming, even if late, even if only with words, even if the cavalry is one person, one poem, one voice refusing to leave.

Issue Three is a book of rooms, rituals, scars, systems, trees, lakes and afterlives. These poems risk form because experience has already broken form open. They do not console, but they do hold. They ask what remains when the body has been marked, when the family has failed, when the room has witnessed, when language is gone or insufficient.

And again and again, in their different ways, they answer: a bit of hope. Not much. But enough to begin.

Max Wallis, May 2026

SECTION I

WHAT DO WE NEED BUT A BIT OF HOPE?

AARON KENT

Night Repairs

I keep a jar of loose minutes on the sill
and rattle it when I feel the urge to scream.
The night is a ball of yarn again,
frayed where the river reaches for the pylons,
taut as we turn off the fridge alarm.

You call from a platform that doesn't exist anymore,
say the train timetables have us scheduled to meet
somewhere south of an epilogue.
I pretend to hear the brakes sing silver on
silver, a promise shaved down to an effigy,
and something inside me throws the switch.

There are names I don't carry out loud,
streets, months, a ferry pulled across chains,
I stack them like postcards facedown
& the past flips through me like a letterbox.

I keep losing buttons down the shower drain.
I keep finding feathers in places without birds.
You tell me that's just how memory works;
a lightbulb threaded through the marble of a tombstone,
a moth practicing thunder without a storm,
the night fixing what it can with what it's lost.

We walk past the mural of a whale
painted on a building thirty miles from the sea.
You say the stars are holes in the blackout curtain
and I swear I've read this in a poem before
so I say, fine, but the light does come through,
even when the stagehands are tired and miss the cue.

I buy a pear from an indoor market and eat it
from the centre out, so I may become a tree one day.
Once I believed trees could hinge open if you leant
in the right place. Once I carried a pocket atlas
and redrew the borders with a flashlight.
Now I keep a small screwdriver in my wallet
for night repairs: the hinge, the atlas, the jar of minutes;
tightened, realigned, enough to see me through

to the day of my underwhelming funeral.

We split at the corner where the grass is actually greener,
and you turn into a streetlight, a reason to keep
me up at night. I turn into a window so you may
pass through me. both of us a signal, both of us safe.

Later, with the central heating on, I'll count
the seconds until the pipes go silent.
If I sleep, I'll dream of a timetable written in pencil,
and your voice smudging me towards an epilogue.

KATIE HALE

Mural

sea spirals around us, swirls into us
on the bypassed wall of the promenade
sea in our bodies, our scales
we summer sea-creatures in this town
that peers bleary from its winter cloud

there's joy in shaking off a mane of kelp and fish
unshelling ourselves in a blue-green blue-grey dive

footsteps on the pavement, click-tap on dry concrete
hoods and collars barricading the cold

below, the puddle wide and undisturbed

o let me smash it
I have been diving towards its dull unruffled surface for so long
and what does a tiled creature yearn for but to shatter?

instead I will slip slight and soundless from the wall
into my waiting reflection
a splashless exit from the world
a splashless entry into the world's waiting mirror

the photographer watches from the bench
in her tattered jacket, clicks the shutter
halfway between one picture and another

What if we kissed inside the taxidermied Gothenburg blue whale?

What if we held each other in the cavernous jaws,
caressed against the tang of stale oil and turpentine?
What if we embalmed ourselves in one another's hands

under the ship-built sternpost, spine and ribs: bodies
inside body; desire inside a yearning for the deep?
What if we, too, let ourselves be beached?

It took two days for their tools to pierce the heart of it,
and then no cart could carry the whole whale at once, no door
in the whole Naturhistoriska Museet was wide enough.

Hush. The stretched skin amplifies each heartbeat like a drum.
Outside, people walk beneath the bones of smaller deaths,
point up at fingerish flippers, the narwhal's mythic horn.

Hold me here in the bulb-lit cavity. This is what I mean
by 'forever': a love so big they tear down walls to let it in.

Rabbit

I come with gloves and balking, with cast-iron shovel kept for these
small untidy deaths – come soon enough the flies are yet to find it –
all but one, crawling the separated snout, scheming with its two front legs –
come soon enough the small black nose could still be twitching
towards distant rain, hot loam of the field – mouth still letting in
the thinnest slip of air – soon enough it steams in unremitting sun,
spongy brown liver, colon sickly pink like a silicon sex toy, spilling
its half-digested mess, a yellow spread among the rich dark auguries:
sultry drops of meat, bulbous excess of gut, wet-look ruffles
in bacchanalian high-fashion – purple, plum, lavender, orchid
gleaming like a fresh coat of varnish – the scattered fur in cut-offs, scraps.
Incredible to think so little skin could hold such life, such lavishness.

HOLLIE MCNISH

in loving memory of the kissing tree

the pale green leaves of the common hawthorn
are often the first to appear each spring
and there we were, almost summer, almost eleven
sunbrellaed by the low white blossom

it took three trips to the tree till i was certain
he smiled each time i shook my head
carved a compass heart in bark instead

for some, it is the may tree,
nicknamed for the month it bloomed
for us, it was the kissing tree, love-shrine
to lips on lips in the woods inside our school

the second time, petal-confetti blessings,
lips ready, i turned my head *'no, sorry'*
'don't worry' he kissed me on the cheek instead

these blossoms were once banned, spring garlands
made for may day celebrations judged unholy crowns
to carnal love by those in power; how strange,
the things we've had forbidden – such fear of flowers

it has been said that the hawthorn
is an unlucky plant to bring into a house;
then again, so much has been said

the third time   *yes*   he checks again   *yes,*
yes   my mouth pressed against his mouth
a softness i still feel
each time the hawthorn bloom is out

my lips are layered now
with many years of grateful kissing
like paintings   painted over paintings

about that first kiss, i don't remember much –
how many seconds we pressed our lips together,
but afterwards, he whispered *'thank you,*
thank you very much'

and set the bar, at ten, forever

OLIVER JAMES LOMAX

Hold This Chicken Whilst I Dance To Smooth Criminal

is what the 12-year-old autistic boy said
with his eyes
in the nonverbal nurture centre
we had been clapping out the poem *Alligator*
by Grace Nichols
and lost in those syllables
he found the confidence and rhythm
to dance towards me with an offering
of a live baby chicken.
So, we both looked on
its panicked heart against my palms
as he moonwalked towards the stars
powering his way through the whole routine,
and I will never unsee
his 45-degree gravity defying lean
how prayer met him in the tilt
and held him there
like the sum of all our will
as if some god had him on a piece of string
his little soul weightless
and tethered to belief.
When I am drained with fear and grief
I carry in my hands the heart of a child
that could not speak.

PETER ARCHER

Apollo 13 Redux

I can't leave my flat today. But the crew
of Apollo 13 knew they'd emerge
from the dark side. And the men
of Apollo 13 heard their hearts beat

before the voice of Mission Control
broke radio silence to tell them
all systems were go and the President
was waiting to talk on the telephone.

As I stand at the door, I'm thinking
of how they scooped up the capsule
from the sea like a hard-boiled egg
and how I can barely bring myself

to stand this side of the fire door
I'm braced behind like the heat shield
that saved the lives of the astronauts.
And I picture the three brave men

waving back from the capsule window
and from the back of an open-top car
as I'm stepping out onto the stairwell
and tuning in to the wild applause

I can hear in my head when I'm out
of my flat at last and I'm thinking
these are the sounds of the world outside
as the astronauts' limo is gliding by

and I watch the spectral motorcade
swept away by flag-waving crowds,
and I'm hanging over a high balcony
wondering how I'll ever get down there.

MELERI DAVIES

Ei rhosod hi[1]

Mae'r rhaw yn torri'r tir
fel cyllell trwy gacen,
pridd yn briwsioni'n aur siwgr brown
wrth godi'r tywyrch yn haul diwedd dydd.
Caea'i ddyrnau am y ddolen,
yn fap pelen bapur o rychau twfn –
hen lwybrau a nentydd
mynydd-dir ei flynyddoedd.

Nid dyma lle mae'n cofio,
mewn gardd lliain bwrdd o betalau
yn fachlud o binc a choch ar ei orwelion.
Ond fama mae o heddiw
yn tawel dendiad ei rhosod hi
gyda gwellaif cneifio.

A fory, bydd yn ôl wrth ei waith,
un rhosyn mewn dŵr ar y silff ben tân
ac yntau allan yn y caeau
yn hel cerrig neu'n agor ffôs,
ei raw yn ddwfn yn y ddaear,
a'r dŵr yn codi i'r wyneb
ac yn llifo

---

1 *Ei rhosod hi* was first published in *Rhuo ei distawrwydd hi, (Cyhoeddiadau'r Stamp)*, November 2024. *This is not where he remembers* is an English translation by the poet for *The Aftershock Review*. *Ei rhosod hi* is included here in Welsh alongside the poet's English translation.

This is not where he remembers

Summer evening in her rose garden,
his shovel cutting through the caked earth.
Golden crumbs of warm soil like sugar
glistening in the end of day sun,
his hand a tight fist on the handle -
a crumpled map of deep furrows, paths and streams
and broken contours of a lifetime on the mountain.

This is not where he remembers,
hunched with scissors now in this table cloth garden
of sunset blooms.
But it is here that he stands today,
pruning her pink roses
un-gloved but with love
in his steel toe capped boots.

Daybreak and his hearth is cold.
Cut glass light shimmering through dust from his mantelpiece
and a single pink rose in clear water embraces another dawn.
This is not where he remembers.

No, he's out in his fields, two feet deep in mountain earth.
The first light splitting heaven and earth
like the igneous rock beneath his feet
breaking with each swing of his pickaxe.
His ditch opening as the earth breathes.
Peat black water rising to the surface.
From this dark opening the water flows
and here he remembers.

RHYS OWAIN WILLIAMS

Document

i.m. my stepfather

The notary public says he needs proof
so I log in to the government's portal,
pay the £11 fee.
When the envelope arrives a week later
I leave it unopened in the hallway.
This is the first time I'll see your death
with my own eyes—
Covid's early unknowns locking each room
your cold body was carried to.
Robbing us of grief's rituals.
Fuelling doubt, thoughts of deception.

When I finally rip the seal,
I learn words I could live without.
Myocardial:
the muscular tissue of the heart.
Atheroma:
fatty deposits in the arteries.
Haemopericardium:
when blood enters where it should not.
Still, though, conspiracy lurks in my peripheries.

It is September, and every birthday card
that drops on my doormat
seems to be written by your hand.
The grass I mowed last week yellows in the sun.
Along the terrace someone sneezes,
and an acoustic guitar is tuned too tight.
The repeated note strains out an open window
to meet another afternoon without you,
the year's last butterflies on the breeze.

Being Less Stressed is on My To-Do List

- ☐ Early morning coffee run—the red-yolk daybreak soundtracked by the hum of a road sweeper.

- ☐ On our doorstep, our neighbour leaves green beans from his allotment, wrapped in old newspaper.

- ☐ Outside the market, the smell of cockles cooking in vinegar and butter enters the bus-stopped bus without a ticket.

- ☐ We circle the bay in the slipstream of quiet tourists, walking through photographs.

- ☐ On the way to the football, we guess what the busker under the railway bridge will be playing. It is always, without fail, 'Going Underground' by The Jam.

- ☐ Sunlight striking the clock tower of Tabernacle Chapel, for a brief moment I see my hometown through my grandfather's eyes.

- ☐ Driving home through the dusk-lit valley, the black hills ripple around us like silkworms, joining our journey towards the sea.

- ☐ *But there's so much to...*

- ☑ Choose something you can always reach for. The weight of keys in your pocket. The fingerprint-sized landing space of your earlobe. The small scar on your palm that looks like your grandmother's initial. The reason why the sound of an owl at night always makes you think of your mother. The way your sons touch their foreheads together when they're tired.

PENNY SHARMAN

Pink Moon

Thursday April 6th 12.34 pm 2023

Pink phlox. I told you I run a little feral around a full one. Sprouting grass moon. It must be a spectacle, huge like our love. Egg moon. If only we'd met sixty years ago, imagine our creation. Fish moon. When we were young, we swam with the dace and minnows. Breaking ice moon. You know when we row, it's like that. Moon when streams become navigable, easy like today's hot sun, your gentle smile. Waking before dawn moon. The papers mention Earth's magnetic core might be to blame. Dreaming of sex moon. When you're young you never think you will lose it and dreaming's not the same. Finding the lost words moon. I wish I had asked mum so much more. Snakes head fritillary moon. Let's not get too Freudian here. Raking dead leaves moon. Back breaking but imagine what lies underneath. Moon when windows open. The illusion of fresh air, even sea air is never dust free. Moon of sticky-buds. I long for the sap, those tiny purple lilac buds hovering inside safety. Moon of patience. Forgetting the losses moon. I never can of course, maybe for a moment, but they will always be here in my mind. A sense of belonging moon. Story of my life, living on the outer edge. Get your head into gear moon and wake up moon. No need for any alarm, the fox and blackbirds never fail, the owl keeps me company. Listen to the copper beech moon. Still shaking the last leaves away. Wild cherry blossom moon. Still waiting for its perfume for bees. Need to aerate the soil moon. I know, I know. Keeping grounded moon. Easier said. Moon of bees returning. I heard a bumble bee today. Moon where you swim in rivers. It's been years, I recall that soft mud between my toes. Moon for opening a heart. Well, that's an easy one for me, how about you? Prayer for the homeless moon. On my knees, can't imagine weather in my bones. Let's shake off the blues moon. Okay, lets. Dancing in the moonlight moon. Isn't that a song? Pay the bloody gas bill moon. Don't make me fume. Moon when owls become quiet. Shush! Moon over the lake of contemplation. A bit of a cliché, isn't it? How long have I got left moon? Nobody knows, nobody knows.

ROBERT HAMBERGER

Writing Hand

It's started to tremble, of its own accord.
A sign of age? Think of all the friends
gone, before any tremor arose.
Salute them, this hand waving them off,
wanting their bright return. So I write here,
every word looping black onto white.
A hummingbird moth quivers at the tips
of valerian. Stalks of Japanese anemone
shiver in the wind. I'm married to each
minute's fluctuation. Do I seek stillness?
If so, I'm backing the wrong horse,
my skittish mare shaking before the race.

In *The Roman Spring of Mrs Stone* I watch
Vivien Leigh's ageing hands. She clenches
them in the betrayal scene – fists
below trembling chin – to stop herself
from falling through the night.
Exquisite unravelling, dark streets
beyond her fingernails, her widow's rings,
catching water from a fountain
to splash one last cold drop
on her forehead before the end.

Let her be a bridge to my writing hand.
It can stroke my husband's stubble,
dive into waves like a guillemot, scribble
a line's agitation, unfurl every finger,
cure itself with rain, the half moons
of each nail old as my skin. It can tremble
to prove I'm alive, rest on this crowded
sheet, motionless as a folded wing.

Instruction to Self

Rise above it, I tell myself.
If I rise, where do I go?
Clouds are too far.

I could walk along
the shore, to clear
my weather,

let every word
drop from my mouth –
pebbles when the tide shifts –

lift my head above
limpets and bladderwrack,
closer to the sky.

I could walk there
and back again,
carry myself like broken

crockery, carefully place
one piece beside another:
rise, shrug, repair.

Afternoon

Our shirts are wrestling with the wind on the line, straining their pegs. Aimlessness draws me into the garden while my husband naps. I notice which roses might benefit from secateurs. I should decide if the oxalis is invasive rather than blooming, whether it needs uprooting, like a tree or a man. Time aggravates the body. My husband says walking takes its toll. Our friend recovers from the after-effects of surgery. She shares new words like *necrotic* and *debride*. Six sparrows at the feeder leave one by one, each checking the air before they fly. I balance this afternoon (including aimlessness, including love) while our socks waver on the line. Our striped arms flail and dance.

ROSIE JACKSON

Hymn to that Night

after Angelo Geter

Praise the trumpet of the student next door
rousing the dead from their slumber. Praise Handel.
Praise Corinthians. Praise the twinkling of an eye.
Praise the stubbornness of breath, the instinct
of hands and feet. Praise the cold night, empty street,
red telephone box. Praise Alexander Graham Bell,
praise the coins in your purse. Praise your friend Geoffrey
for picking up, praise his SAAB that speeds through the city
like a clouded leopard. Praise the doctors who shake
their heads at despair. Praise the stomach pumps.
Praise the invisible hands, floor-moppers, tea makers,
toilet cleaners. Praise the rails round the bed, their mirage
of a cross. Praise the other women on the ward,
praise the mothers, praise your courage. Praise
your sleeping children. Praise your stolen children.
Praise the bruises. Praise the unanswered prayers.
Praise the darkness that folds its arms against you.
Praise the gatekeepers who know this is not your hour.
Praise the spring morning that opens like a tired eye,
the daffodils that girdle the ancient walls. Praise
the thousands of days left to you. Praise the angels
who know how to push you back into your young body.
Yes, praise your young body. Praise the trumpet that sounds.

RACHEL BURNS

Marsden Rock

Walking past Souter Lighthouse
along the coastal path
a brown stoat with a white chest
runs across the path – I point it out
but too late as it disappears into the bushes
– the day is one of the brightest – early spring
still cold with an offshore breeze. I want to tell you
something. We walk past the cliff edge –
small memorials pinned to railings
fake plastic flowers, heart -shaped plaques,
photographs, young men, some dads –
smiling faces before things got bad,
a mother's handwritten note –
I say I wonder why choose a cliff edge
maybe it's the dramatic.
I want to tell you something.
Earlier I'd sat in the doctor's office
& said I'm feeling like I'm falling off the edge of a cliff
& she tiptoed around some questions on my mental health,
something I never did in my old job
one girl told me she thought about
killing herself all the time
& she found it annoying –
another found themselves returning, again & again
to the same suicide spot –
another rang me to say he was going to kill himself
jumping in front of a train
& / or walking to the petrol station
pouring petrol over himself
& setting himself on fire
We stand & stare at Marsden Rock
the flock of black cormorants perched on top.
I say the doctor gave me a note to say I'm not fit to work
you still don't ask –

HELEN MORT

The Juniper Tree

Germany. A wealthy couple pray every day for God to grant them a child.
    In their courtyard is a huge evergreen, starred with blue berries. Juniper.

In winter, beneath its branches, the wife peels an apple. She cuts her finger
    and drops of blood fall onto the snow. A month later, she gives birth

to a baby boy as white as snow and as red as blood. She dies of happiness.
    The husband buries her under the juniper.

The new wife is not interested in trees. She loves morning sex and steak
    cooked rare, glasses of Merlot soupy and warm as blood, the scent

of smoke on her clothes. She wears a strong perfume that some say
    reminds them of garlic. They have a child, a daughter. The stepmother

only likes her stepson when he frowns and looks like his father.
    When she decapitates the boy, there is surprisingly little mess

and the head rolls across the floor like a marble. So she gathers it up,
    binds it to the rest of his body with a bandage and props his body

onto a chair outside, with an apple resting on his lap. Later,
    she's at the kitchen counter with a butcher's knife, turning him

into "blood-soup". When her husband comes home, they eat it
    together. The bones are buried under the Juniper tree.

That night, under the ground, in the shelter of the tree, the bones
    fuse together in the shape of a bird. There is a fine mist in the air

and the bird looks spectral as it burrows out of the ground, launches,
    wings tipped purple and blue, chest the colour of a bruise.

Its eye is a juniper berry. It darts towards the town and as the sun rises,
    it sings its life for all to hear.

SECTION II

AN ANTHROPOLOGY OF GRIEF

CATHERINE REDFORD

An Anthropologist's Catalogue of Death Rituals

Lay her on a mountaintop, buried in the sky as alms
for the birds. After forty days, she will be transformed
into a wild swan; collect graveyard nettles, if you wish,
to break the enchantment, but know she will always
be left with one wing.

There must be no canopic jar for the heart;
this should be stored in the secret compartment
of your writing desk. Bandage it in strips torn
from her love letters, choosing only lines written
in the present tense.

Put on your veil and go tell the bees of her death,
the news hanging above their hives like smoke,
like an accusation you wish you'd never made. Watch
the swarm form a cloud, expand like a growth,
a storm vibrating against its limits.

Come the spring, plant wildflower seeds in the compost
made from fifty-one bunches of anniversary roses
never given. Tend to them like children, choosing only
the most beautiful to pull from the ground and strew
on her grave, where they will wilt within the day.

Instruct AI to create her portrait afresh each morning,
changing nothing. Watch as she morphs into an urn,
a mushroom, a yew tree, an owl. Take the feathers
she sheds and tuck them in the pages of the book she left
half-read on her bedside table.

Auction off her unused future in miscellaneous lots,
then lock yourself in the empty house, swallowing the key.
Become obsessed with preservation: make jams,
can fruit. Line up the jars on shelves down in the cellar,
ready for the world to end, again.

Things I wasn't prepared for when she died

how I'd get home from her funeral and want to tell
her all about it / that I'd buy her favourite food for
months afterwards / not knowing whether to write
wife or widow when I signed the forms / so many
forms / the brief catharsis of sorting her belongings
/ expeditions to charity shops desperate to buy
back her clothes / the homesickness of grief / the
unsettling moment I realised I'd been mourning
her long before she'd died / how it's not so much
the looking back that's painful but the glances to
the side / the ghostly life running parallel with my
own / the life that could have been / caught in a
flash from the corner of my eye

Postscript: I return to the river one year after her death

Choose your own journey on or in or beside the water:
If you are reading this and you are lost, go to (a)
If you are reading this and you are yearning, go to (b)
If you are reading this in the company of ghosts, go to (c)

(a)
like retrieving those treasures that slipped under floorboards |
surface light filtering | recategorising | pebbles rust bones weed
mud mud mud sludge bubbles decomposition the forgotten |
washing & revealing | lifted to meet the day | recovering

(b)
there are quick rumours of rain from upstream | fallingfalling |
sending the silt giddy | rearranging | atomic vibrations of a half-
remembered song | furrowing & unearthing | the glints
oh the glints | silent darkness that follows a blown bulb |
snowdrops under the willow | deep loam scent | life submerged
| untended | fleeting | your kingdom of the found

(c)
strain against the carving of the land | press | a lover's obsession
| fold into a thruppence folk-tale | night-watched and weighed
down by a pocketful of rocks | tripped by the hagstone | hauled
onto the banks | the water loosens and laughs | erosion-exposed
secrets | she never told you | and you'll never know why

GEMMA STRANG

the weight of a heart

my father's post-mortem of 1994 says
The heart weighed 481g

my mother's post-mortem of 2017 says
The heart weighed 322g

stats that slap
like meat on metal
cold and nothing and everything

family trivia you can't easily drop into conversation

'what did your parents do?'
'well, they carried 803g of heart between them, that's for sure'

nobody should know the sum
of a loved one's body parts

coroner-bothering deaths
bad enough
without this dossier
of body bits
gram by gram;
a recipe
for a diabolical stew

grisly data weighing
on the living, now

but it's the hearts that haunt

481g
322g

pathologist, tell me

how much space did I occupy in there?

scalpelly speaking –
a steak or a sliver?

of those hard-knocked hearts
(despite what you read)

On incision, no scars to the heart were seen

of those magician hearts
capable, sometimes
of vanishing acts

of all those grams

how many were mine?

things that also weigh 322g

when you learn from the coroner's report
that your mother's heart
weighed *322g*

the obvious thing to do with the data
is to google

average heart size woman

and lay to rest
whether her heart
was bigger or smaller
than the average
motherheart

part of you can't

the same part, perhaps
that already knows

somehow the easier thing to do, one saturday afternoon
is google

things that weigh 322g

which is how you learn

a 4-pack of Tesco almond croissants
46 pieces of prehistoric pottery unearthed at an archaeological investigation
at the Darlow's Depot Site, Fengate, Peterborough
adidas SolarGlide running shoes
a tortoiseshell kitten found dumped in a pine forest on the corner of the
Glencoe/Kongorong turn-off in south-east Australia
a rare 1969 sterling silver Guernsey milk can jug
a sharing pouch of Starburst

all weigh the same
as your mother's heart
once did

my favourite way to remember you

is all of us agog
while you tell us a funny story
a pratfall, usually yours

The mouth and tongue were normal

all of us
in the palm of your hand
too rapt to spot the life line

Manner of death: Unnatural

your eyes
your lilt
alight and alive
and us hanging
on every word

Ligature abrasion around neck

oh
the fervour
as you approach
punchline glory
oblivious to the tiny blob of peanut butter
on the world's softest cheek

Striae gravidarum were noted over the abdomen

how
the marks we leave
on each other

stay

NICKY KIPPAX

Platitude Bingo

<table>
<tr><td>God never gives you more than you can handle</td><td>Hold on to all the precious memories</td><td>She’s in a better place</td><td>Everything happens for a reason</td></tr>
<tr><td>I know exactly how you feel</td><td>She’s watching over you</td><td>Good will come from this in time</td><td>At least she’s not suffering anymore</td></tr>
<tr><td>Stay strong</td><td rowspan="2" colspan="2">FREE SQUARE

(Take a break)</td><td>This too will pass</td></tr>
<tr><td>You must move on</td><td>Heaven has a new angel</td></tr>
<tr><td>She wouldn’t want you to be sad</td><td>It was her time</td><td>Be grateful you had the time you did</td><td>Worse things happen at sea</td></tr>
<tr><td>Don’t choose to be unhappy</td><td>Time heals all wounds</td><td>We have no words</td><td>God needed her more than you did</td></tr>
</table>

SALLY READ

Instructions for the Scattering of Ashes

Brace as they hand you the box: it's not
the teacup full of dust you imagined.
The weight's more like stuffed grouse,
and potatoes for peeling. Steel yourself,
too, for how much there is: six flour-bags
full, and where would you put it? It'll fall
like cement dust on the field where he played,
and you find yourself wishing for rain,
but know that this (like flour, like cement)
will not wash away. Remember that avoiding
the spiritual was his aim (and yours)
but be aware that as you lift up the lid
ashes will rise, become the smoke of an altar,
a weather phenomenon, or the sign
of a fire, that you wave with your hands
but can't quell. A breeze, then, is worse:
he cleaves to jeans, boots, is caught in eyelashes
and hair, the hall of your throat, so,
in the lane where he drank from a stream,
you hawk like a builder covered in dust,
wheeze like a man who has shouldered
the wounded. Note: at the risk of coating
the whole village in dun-coloured snow,
you'll bring the rest of him home. You thought
he would mimic the turf as you folded him in,
but he billows out from the hole like the ghost
you refuse to believe in. You rub your hands,
blink, bang the emptied box on the side —
Is that it? Is it all gone? Are you sure?
You won't see the dog and the night deer
drawn to the spot, sniffing not death, nor life,
but something between: a rupture in the night's
scent, a decimated presence, a dry patch
like Gideon's in the cloak of dew on the lawn.

Dead Man's Tambourine

As you typed, the mirrors flashed with London light,
the plane trees flared the belly of their leaves,
and the tambourine was hooked above your head,
like a rifle mounted on a wall. Music was your other beast—
the sliding blues of harmonica, the tambourine's
teeth trembling like an aspen's silver, instead

of words like these I drunk-fight to tell the breath
of you gone dead. If I could write you back
(the music, listening smoke and mirth), but
death is the tambourine laid low on
the rotten piano, the daylight's lack, the tin
discs rigidly apart as a pair of aching teeth.

CLARE BEST

Stop the world

I want to get off, my mother would say
with a chuckle. Sometimes
I thought she meant it.

Did she plan to disappear?
She practised every day –
standing empty-handed, gazing

into middleness, or through a window
towards an invisible sea.
I was only eight, but knew

she had made herself
brave enough to tell the world
to stop – so she could fall

into starry darkness,
watch this blue-green bauble
spin away.

ghostly email to my mother

I have you   as a curious line
of question marks   your letters
beside me   your face   in my reflection

I thought you'd like to know   your youngest
found the car you loved   bought it back
twenty-five years after you died

fitted new hub caps   steering wheel
oh yes   we miss you   even when
you were here   we missed you like hell

I study scraps of your life   not to
shape remnants   into a whole   no
no   I do it   to honour   the gaps

typing words   into the keyboard   I notice
they haven't appeared   on the screen

Guttering

First, from the safety of the ground, I try to clear
the gutter with a broom – on tiptoe, swearing
as I prod and lift, broom-end clanking

on zinc – until I realise a ladder and hands
will do the job better. Serious now, I pull on hat
and gloves, push phone into pocket, just in case.

Dusk – blackbird song, pale stars, a sketchy moon –
I walk the ladder along the house, check footings,
climb, drop wet-dry oak leaves into heaps.

A polished crescent hangs among brilliant stars:
the house and I – prepared for rain, wind, the last
of the leaves, and night. Whatever must come.

STEPHEN BOYCE

Hinged

Behind what once was the railway station,
in all that remains of Bucha's Yablunka Street,

apartment blocks, collapsed nests now, are waiting
for signs of movement under the steady beat

of spring rain, its pitter-pat on burnt-out cars,
on exposed baths and shattered basements

where everything lies scattered – dogs and toys,
a suitcase, phone lines, Uncle Babak's beard.

One by one figures venture out. Heads bowed
and hands to mouths, they scan the stricken heaps,

when some gentle voice remarks that what sounds
like the creaking hinge of a metal gate

is in fact the urgent and insistent plea
of a great tit yet to find a mate.

Minding the Gap

Begin with a mother who's dying – will be gone in a breath,
        or its lack. Remember each detail of habit,
demeanour or dress. Surely you know this?

Recall, too, the back story, the convent school days,
        frost on the inside of windows in winter,
and surgical corsets, and driving on beaches.

Then notice the gap she will leave in her going,
        a small but significant gap of something like love.
She was one more speck of light on a hill

from where you were then. To her you were too close for comfort.
        Now it's all teeth and spectacles and pills
– you've fallen headlong into the gap, its more than momentary

hesitation.   Surely you know this.
        No matter.   Persist.

Late Conversation

And when, to the steady tolling
    of a solitary bell,
the Danes had all assembled
    in their generations – greybeards
and those with down on their lip –
    and each had embraced the other
in peace and consolation
    as the light of the seven days
fell upon them and the thanksgiving
    flowers guided their step,
they turned and together raised up
    the burning boat and cast it adrift
on the tide of its own great silence.
    And they knew in their hearts then
that the songs they sang, the poems
    they read and the myths they told
that day, were not the terms
    of some bargain with God,
they were simple expressions of love,
        for you, Inger.

DARAGH BYRNE

I Was There When My Father Died

After Sharon Olds

All winter he withered with the sun,
all winter I watched him eaten from inside,
his dead-balloon skin tightening against his ribs,
his translucent grin thinning into his face.
All winter I counted the acorns of my heart
hoping they might sustain me
through the shortening days
because I knew I would be there
when he died. That mid-December morning—
decorations left in boxes, presents still unbought—
my mother was there, my brother, my sisters,
the woman who was my wife: all of us there
at that still moment when he went still
before the keening rose from us
and fused into the air of him rising.
How I wanted to jump into his lungs,
how I wanted to reach out of him
and pull his air back in.
How I wanted to be there.
How I still want to be there.

BLAKE MORRISON

Hungerford Bridge

Lost among the crowds on Hungerford Bridge -
commuters on mobiles, late sun in their hair -
you wonder how you've ended as you are,

not from dismay that you might have done better
but bemusement at the choices you've made,
or the choices made for you, or how you slid

from grabbing what you wanted to something
more equable, not a shot at eminence
but a workaday, unhindered existence,

dusk through the window lighting the shelves
with books you've read or haven't got round to,
and happiness, which you can't put in words.

Elsewheres

'There isn't a train I wouldn't take,
No matter where it's going.'

Edna St Vincent Millay

Who will take me to the crying of the waters?
Oh for one salt smell of the sea once more,
the sappy heave, the blue and bitter fall
and the coast's last fisherman in oilskins.

Who will sit with me anywhere but here?
If not the sea, maybe a hayfield in August
or curlews calling from the moor-side
and a jam-jar of raggedy cornflowers.

By the pool

On our way to the bar we saw
the white sheet – her partner of fifty years
they said, taking his usual dip.
Not a bad way to go we said,
raising a glass to him.
Death is for others.
You know it hasn't happened to me yet.
I'd have told you about it if it had.

DR ANNA PERCY

Ink Plush Succulents

After Song of the Gourd C.D Wright

I am falling apart [] keeping succulents alive is easy [] they thrive on neglect [] bar the bijoux cacti [] whose spines wilted into a desiccated husk [] after six months behind the nautical curtain [] the jade plant that wanders etiolated towards the sunlight [] has survived since I moved in [] I am falling apart [] though less dramatically than I thought [] the ultrasound of my shoulder [] where the tendon snaps over my scapular [] tendinopathy [] I do not need a shoulder replacement [] the succulents leaves may shrivel if I go away for weeks [] they suck up the water on my return [] replump [   ] in the hands of the disconcertingly attractive physio I might learn how not to fall apart [] keeping succulents alive is one of the only constants [] besides writing poetry in my entire life [   ] in these past two months of falling apart [] the little finger tendons being reattached [] the codeine pain fog [] I was banned from writing for the first time since my manic psychotic episode [] the graphomania [] wallsbedsheetsjeans [] I was falling apart [] being unable to get ink on my skin [] like the jade plants sucking up my guilty belated watering in their phloem [] I am replumping with ink [   ] did not have time to walk through All Saints park [] will stop later to investigate the trees in Whalley Range [] trees I really should know the name of by now [] have held onto leaves [] a washed out old paperback page yellow [] hordes of them still clinging to branches [] the weather by turns frozen and mild must have caused this [] saw a fox [] the other night [] my body has lurched without warning [] like every other awesome autumn slump into being nocturnal with a slow right hand [] something had to give today [] I forwent a hair dryer and the bus [   ] the sky the kind of blue it has not been in weeks [] cumulus puffs of cloud that cannot be rain [ ] even though one walked off [] my compost bin in its jaws I still thrilled to see a fox [] an adolescence without spotting a single brushtail will do that to a person

In 2006 I had a T-Shirt That Said DEATH BEFORE DISCO and Now I Regret it

For Jo Rose D. 2024

Donna Summer is whirling psychedelic through MacArthur Park ▯ in my ear ▯ a bitter wind threatens to take my PVC peaked cap ▯ shakes the petals from the magnolia tree with the fairy lights▯ I thought were blinking a message meant only for me ▯ when I was manic ▯ a scarcity darkened pasted to the pavement ▯ by footsteps [ ] fragile early spring has cooled ▯ I cannot remember if I ever talked Disco with you ▯ after the funeral ▯ where I sat outside the crematorium ▯ with the crowd who loved you ▯ so loved you ▯ they overflowed the chapel ▯ watering the rose garden with saline ▯ held the hand of a woman ▯ who was there when you first picked up a guitar ▯ I told your sister ▯ I wept buckets to the James Taylor song chosen ▯ was internally amused because you knew I hated him ▯ because my mother loved him ▯ you said I should change my mind [ ] I meant I loved you ▯ that talking music with you was mind expanding ▯ you made me laugh ▯ you have no mind left to change ▯ I hope to change mine dozens of times ▯ I saw your sisters teeth mirrored your own ▯ I did not tell her how yours split a pill in two ▯ at the final rave in the disused swimming pool ▯ of the leisure centre ▯ boldened by chemicals ▯ I told my lover ▯ I loved him for the first time for the second time ▯ him finding it adorable ▯ I forgot ▯ is exactly why our love is like the songs of Bill Callahan▯ the beauty is in the wonk ▯ last year my sole filling from youthful bravado opening beer bottles ▯ with my molars crumbled ▯ the tree outside my kitchen window ▯ overlooked by the awry jade plant ▯ has been shook of the blossom reminiscent of the hailstones ▯ I slept through ▯ the stained glass ship window ▯ on the house at the corner of Brantingham road ▯ has been replaced by UPVC [ ] when I lit a candle for you ▯ in Norwich Cathedral ▯ wept behind a pillar ▯ I saw myself at twelve ▯ bored by grandeur of the stonework ▯ engrossed in Rats of Nimh ▯ waiting to sing with the school choir ▯ the word misericord rang through my brain today ▯ I do not want to think about time ▯ I want to think about love ▯ and your gentle laugh

SECTION III

THE REAR BEDROOM

ABEER AMEER

The Rear Bedroom (13 x 17 ft) of House 2, Haditha, a Town by the Euphrates River, Iraq, 19th November 2005

after photograph taken by Lance Corporal Andrew Wright, Olympus digital camera

i)

There is the mother, Ayda, on the bed surrounded
by her children. They're all in their nightclothes;
pyjamas, *dishdasha*. All of them have been shot
dead. All shot at close range.
All of them shot in the head.

Ayda is on her back, on the right side of the bed.
She's wearing a brown velvet *dishdasha.*
Her head wrapped in a white towel.
She's on the right side of the bed. Maybe she was shot first.
At the head of the bed there are shelves
within the wooden headboard.

On the middle shelf, at the centre,
there is a closed, blood-spattered
Quran
on a book stand.

ii)

Next to Ayda is her son, eight-year-old Mohammed.
He's face down on the bed, wearing an olive-green

thick tracksuit. November mornings can be very cold, here.
His elbow is near his mother's lap.

And there, in the foreground, is five-year-old Zaynab,
she's wearing colourful Mickey Mouse pyjamas.

Her head has been shattered, there's very little of it left.
She was probably standing when she was shot.

Part of her brain is on her brother's tracksuit bottoms.

There is no blood on the yellow blanket next to her.

Sabaa, aged ten, is at the top left corner of the bed.
Half on the bed, half off the bed.

Her leg is trapped in position by fifteen-year-old Noor,
who is crouched on her hands and knees on the floor

between the bed and the wall.
There is a lot of blood and brain tissue on the wall.

There is blood and brain tissue
on Noor's rose dishdasha; it's Zaynab's.

iii)

And there, at the top of the bed, there is Ayesha,
the youngest. Three-years-old. She's wearing
a royal blue and white top with a flower in the centre.
Her hand is close to Mohammed's head.
The left side of her face rests on the bed.
A stream of blood on her right cheek.

> *It looks like there's a bullet hole in the pinna of her ear.*
> *There is possible stippling*
> *but no further investigation was permitted.*

The number 12 written on her cheek
in red Sharpie marker.

The Haditha Massacre Photos that the Military Didn't Want the World to See:
Madeline Baran, The New Yorker, 27th August 2024

Wild Grass: Mahmudiyah, Iraq, 12th March 2006

The boys come home from school.
They find their house in the orchard
of date palms and pomegranates,
in flames. They run
to their uncle's house
as smoke fills the air
with the smell of propane
and burnt meat.

Inside the walls are the bodies
of their parents and sisters.
A bullet ridden family.
In the bedroom, their mother
on the ground, broken arms, a crater
in her chest,
and their six-year-old sister,
the girl named after
the sound of water,
who loved to play hide and seek,
still grasping wild grass in her hand.
Her face – blown off.
Their father in a pool of blood
in the corner of the room,
splatter covering the wall behind him.
Shot in the head.
In the next room, the older sister,
the beautiful daughter, the one named
after the perfume of flowers.
The girl who had dreams
of living in the city.
Fourteen years young.
She's on the ground,
one leg stretched, the other bent,
her dress lifted up to her neck.

Kerosene was poured
to start the flames at her face.
and divert blame.
It must have been insurgents.

While back at the checkpoint
two hundred yards away
the US soldiers who did this,

who hatched their plan
over a game of cards, whiskey
and energy drink mix, celebrate
with grilled chicken wings.
In the highest of spirits
that what they've just done
is *totally awesome.*

This darkness

has no edges
no sides to hold
no patches to catch
    and peel back

it is black ink   in fresh water
turning a clear path into raven
pecking at earth to a prompt burial

its dull ache digs with each heartbeat
            foretelling   foreboding
pleuritic in its letters.

There is an end to this covering, somewhere.
Or, so they say.

ÖZGE LENA

Bloodstones

The bombings were just around
the corner and the water wars

were about to start.
A week before you died,

we were walking on the beach,
the sea a deep mirror

of the acidic sunset sky.
We were listing the things

we found that weekend—a baby
crab in the dark eye hole

of a teddy bear. A silk tuft of hair
with a piece of pink scalp.

The body of a seagull wrapped
in strings. A jar of milk

teeth adrift in rose water.
Bloodstones. Burst plastic boats.

The amputated arm
of a wooden marionette, waving.

A tiny red shoe, shiny like the one
in our empty cradle.

I held it out to you. You said
life was always possible.

I pressed it on my cesarean scar
as a missile slashed the leprous sun.

1001 Paintings

She dresses the fresh cut on the leg
of her easel with a tight knot, she knows
that her emperor knows nothing about dreams.

They have sharp-tipped black wings.

She dresses the cut on her arm then,
a red emblem appears on the gauze bandage
for a high price she has already paid.

For two years and nine months, one day left.

She bleeds out of the door before dawn,
a thin tatterdemalion spirit
taking her colours away from evil.

Who isn't dead, untoxic pills, he's dead asleep.

She goes up to the cliff, places a blank canvas
on the lame easel, on her palette are all
shades of black within the hues of a new sun.

Around her, the day breaks open like a pink promise.

Dark-feathered beings cluster over
the abyss as she paints and paints, proud number
1001 glistens at the back of this painting.

She paints like Scheherazade tells her stories.

SECTION IV
THE HAPPINESS BUSINESS

ADRIAN SLATCHER

Why the Old Songs, Nanna?

It is the mirror that stands between
the pages of our parallel lives –
like a Chinese screen, reminiscent of Whistler's room
the Princess from the land of porcelain,
chipped cup that we sip a hot drink from,
bare floor-tiles, just washed,
and strips of newspaper, blotting paper pathway
I'm permitted to walk across,
to hover on one leg, turn and swivel,
I have a pelican's legs, wrapped under me;
the potion – I remember now - hot Ribena
the only thing that could soothe away my cough
and stood there, lolling boy, no more than seven
asking too many questions,
starting on stories that hadn't an ending...

Or did you wish me away, this one time
so you could get down on your hands and knees?
In your eighth decade, white-haired
scullery maid; what pennies you earned.
I would be given free run of the library,
the brown-fringed books on big game hunting,
the type tipping down the page in endless columns,
an occasional linocut of a lion or a buffalo;
who knew the world had such horrors in it
and so many crimes confessed to?
At your kitchen table colouring fish
in the multiple colours of the felt-pen pack
and give them names; all forgotten; creating
a unity I would never quite achieve,
singing along to the radio and asking;
why the old songs nanna?

The Happiness Business

We had to re-learn happiness,
my family, and having once been happy
knew we could be again,
but like a skill you once had
to perfectly cross a ball
or craft a particularly elaborate stitch
the re-learning was beyond us,
compared with how easy the first time.

They called me a "happy chappy",
and then too, that stopped;
and I found a picture of my mother
on the cusp of girlhood, laughing,
and wish these versions of us
could return; but so tangled up
is our happiness in our loss
that we can no longer reconstruct it
from the few clues we've got.

Toby Jug

Each time I passed Victoria Park that summer
I took a photograph of the river,
to show you that outside the hospital
the world remained. I once thought that faced with death
I would request a final trip to see the north sky
and it would be enough. Now I know the cruelty
of illness – that it takes away even that hope –
safe and fed, but trapped in a bland room
devoid of personalisation. No wonder you think of home,
no wonder you ask to go home, no wonder each visit
I want to bring you something from there,
a "Lilliput Lane" house or Toby jug,
something to hold on to when memory falters.
A year later, I have one wish:
I would take a picture of the river
and you would be there to see it.

BENEDICTA NORELL

The Jar and the Scar

Nil by mouth the sign said.
I was a good reader, already
losing reality in story books,
my favourite way to dissociate.
Appendix is quite a long word
and the others got ice cream.

I don't recall who it was, doctor,
nurse, showed me the organ after,
a green/black worm, trapped
or a little finger withering away.
I suppose some kids loved the jar
or why present it with such relish?
That ugly thing had been taken
from my cut-up body. What else
was in there waiting to kill me?

Just one more way to be different,
like the scar, so red, sewn up tight
with barbed wire, spiked with blood.
White now, an unfamiliar winter.

They Came for Me

They came for me
before birth, with a jeep,
at birth, with the cord
wrapped around my neck,
in those early years,
with the labour of adults
and vats of guilt for drowning.
Later, with lust, misplaced
and thrust into my throat.
They gave me big jobs
with their eyes on my chest,
while the mind recorded,
undisturbed and gathering.
They came for me with drinks
spiked with frothing expectation
of service and energy transfer.
I failed to fulfil their orders
and they came for me again,
with words from another century,
scarlet woman, terrible mother,
departing empty-handed at last.

Hubba Bubba

Mother, I remember
all those times
you used to say,
if I ever grew up
to have a husband,
he would, one day,
be sure to leave me.

Mother, I remember
how you used to know
that meant I would
have to work, like you.

Mother, I remember
that you used to claim
my fictitious future children
as your compensation.

It's those words that stick
like chewed up
Hubba Bubba
bubble gum
on the scrawled underside
of a classroom desk.

That need for *compensation*
for only having me.

DAN O'BRIEN

Your Confirmation

the stone walls embracing a family of strangers
the elderly the ill the heart savaged the insane
the yawning fathers and scented grim mothers
the patches of baldness and scrublands of gray
the dandruff on shoulders a louse on the nape
the breasts of damp-haired girls in stiff dresses
the wool slacks constraining painful erections
the stained-glass iridescence of flesh and fire
the ancient rector helixing into his bony pulpit
the rafters above like our galleon has capsized
the seraph's wings enveloping my eyes within
the premonition of a photograph of you after
the ceremony outside where you weep before
the black oaken door and the rose thorn bush

1985

This was before. The four of us gathered around a big box like a campfire in the unfinished room. Squatting on a floor of splintering plywood; the new electric baseboard heaters unwired, switches pointless, thermostat blank, paneling off-gassing, recessed sockets gaping. We could see our breathing in the red-and-green glamour of the festooned hedges outside curtainless windows reflecting the shimmering silvery tinsel on the tree behind us. Christmas Eve. The box was wrapped in candy stripes. We wondered what it was and who from but nobody had a clue. Not our clever elder sister, home from school; not our quiet brother and not you, our almost unspeakable brother. The truth was only three of us believed in the unfinished room, the wrapped box, the anticipation of our lives in the morning. Because you were lying, you knew what was concealed inside: the merciless gift of your suicide.

TOM BRANFOOT

Mother Triptych

1.

she was fine   by which I mean
she sustained

no lasting injuries
I floated   on the landing

pigeon-chested
one afterschool evening   chambered

by divorce   in isolate rooms
someone must have rung

an ambulance   at an unwound
hour   of a flowerless month

I would have helped her   will have
shadowed   and waited

for discharge   reckoning feathers
palmed blister packs

2.

buckling into the wall   you spill
my minor life

from the rim   of your cup
I want to peace the smashed plates

squeezed words
like toothpaste   unputbackable

who am I to say   you faith
the wrong things

that credibility   means more
than dinner from the floor

3.

your third christmas alone
capillaries   roquefort-veined

in stale columbaritude
silvered beloved   smoked out

vermin   I never understood it
we oscillate between villainy

nests laid bare   by varicose trees
farmers tender fire to pallets

garden waste   manure
our new house in the pasture

seasons blur   in television blue
sculpted from leather   and grief

bats varnish   the night orchard
I count each tectonic breath

memory is kind   a kind
of unlistening

SECTION V

WHAT ELSE IS A BODY FOR?

ELIZABETH EGER

MRI

Rolled
from a trolley
into a tunnel where sound waves
will pummel thoughts into images.
Headphones on to muffle
extreme noise. I see
my self un
ravelling – an old cassette ribbon
shaken off its spool and
tangling into knots so
tight that
all trace of music is erased or smudged
into one unholy hiss.
How does the brain appear?
Like the s h i m m e r i n g l i e of a mirage on the
freeway? Like the
fretwork of a ruined tree?
The contortions of a coral reef or the dimples on
orange peel?
These are my thoughts – surfacing,
silent, intermittent holes
of blue unseen
and uncollected.
The contours are etched and
the rough music ends.
I am released
from ultra violet
into the quiet yellow
of the day's close.
'You can stand up now,
but m o v e
s l o w l y.'

HILARY HARES

Blue Badge

I'm at the chemist
in the Jag. Beside me
on the seat a cardboard box:
inside the pethidine
and methadone
which didn't touch the pain
and all the hyped-up pills
which haven't worked.

The duty doctor last called in
at 4.03 a.m.
and what he said was right,
and now you're gone,
my only thought is
that I just can't bear
to share the house with
four long years of failed hope.

It's barely light: 5 minutes left
before the 'Open' sign will turn,
and yet the car park's full –
the last disabled bay
my only choice.
Thank heavens, then,
for your Blue Badge, a Godsend
when you lost the strength to walk.

I park, pick up the box
and head towards
the chemist's door.
Before I've taken twenty steps
a woman in a steel-grey 4x4
jumps out and snaps:
You can't park there, there's
nothing wrong with you.

ANGI HOLDEN

The Parameters of Radiance

Three small marks, one on each hip,
one on his belly, set the coordinates.
In the half light of a November afternoon
they are little more than freckles
against his pale skin, as if exposed to summer.

The ink's stain, hidden from sight,
will last through his remaining days,
a shadowy reminder of darkness,
of sleepless nights, of the muted glow
of streetlamps glimpsed through curtains,
of the small arch of morning over the sill.

MAURA DOOLEY

Acute

The line of trust runs at 45°,
the point of intersection changing

from nursery to nursing home,
via hospital where a flask,

suspended,
pumps its goodness into a tired hand.

Wire, tube, cord, your outstretched arm,
the many accents of love.

JESSICA MOOKHERJEE

Cows

I almost call you to say stay, but don't.
Two cows in a field, pressed close.
Hail stutters the car home when I see them.
Back in the bar, green tea between us.
You said yes to a few hours. I said nothing.
I wanted to be inside your life.
A shutter fell. You thinned into landscape,
a gap in the trees. You didn't ask
how I'd been, if the drugs were working.
Your child was awake all night, you said,
told her facts about marmosets, quail,
how cows choose one friend and stay—
facts about marmosets, quail
to quiet a child who won't sleep.
If the drugs were working, how I'd been—
you didn't ask. A gap in the trees,
you thinned into landscape. A shutter fell.
Inside your life, I said nothing.
I wanted you to stay. You said
a few hours. Back in the bar,
green tea between us.
Hail stutters the car home when I see them.
Two cows in a field, pressed close.
I almost call you to say *stay*, but don't.

Sub-optimal

I'm connected to my womb. The night something lived inside me I saw green lights
when I closed my eyes, chanted, *please please go away, come to earth some other way*.
It's all hit and miss. I read that a fox's uterus can show signs of both her aborted
and birthed cubs. Ten percent of mammal foetuses don't make it out. Resorption.

When I studied for my masters I learned that a foetus can be reabsorbed
by the womb in a sub-optimum environment. When is it a good time?
Living in a bomb site, my father wouldn't lend me the money for the mortgage.
Lead, mercury, nickel and manganese; these send signals to terminate.

KATRINA MOINET

Mother Vérité and Mary Wollstonecraft Clear me a Plinth for Menopause's Final Gift

what else is a body for? i ask my shatterproof self on day seven of a bleed which is day 35 / or perhaps day 63 / of a pregnancy i never knew i was carrying

people who live in glass houses / should never throw caution to an empty wind / or take part in wild unprotected sex / declares the (female) GP / who'll reprimand me / in her sterile office / on day 23 of a haemorrhage that's maybe day 50 / of a pregnancy i never knew i was (mis)carrying

what else is a body for? but to house memory / where memory is the lost baby slipping from me / a half-truth slithers away / leaves me tightrope walking / unanchored

what was my body thinking? throwback to sweet sixteen / self-hauntings from all the unplanned futures / pregnancies that never came / but a fear remained / my entire life / how to survive this lottery of misfired ejaculations / worn down by a rhythm this single threaded thought / how a single man could bring me down / with the split of a single condom

scant explanation / for not recognising / my curved glass aperture could still house / life / after ivf / this shuttered shop's shut / i'd declared so many times and laughed / too many times

a new failing of mine / doubt in the persistent power of a menopausal womb / which digs down into toiled soil / furrows purges / all the blooms / always intended to fall

so i sit bone cold / as the porcelain warms / and watch between thighs / fist-sized clots evacuate / then i know / this is no day-seven bleed / nor a ten-day bleed / nor the nineteen-day bleed it becomes / but the grief-relief of losing an unplanned baby / and the unplanned baby / being first to let me know

The body as protest

A Shovel between the Sheets, after Joelle Taylor

Sleepless in snakeskin leather, compressed next to you
pricked skin clings to cool silk. I'm boiling up but you don't
notice   how I wear
nipples knuckle-hard, my pale heart on your ironed sleeve we make up
cat-n-mouse games of who'll touch who first who's first to
sling spitfire starter-gun sparks which prove
love lingers longer than desire; but twenty-five years on you
don't even know the difference; have
you ever considered their similarity is not
flesh bound but a grinding mind made
alive with fresh wet night thoughts of anything
anything at all that might keep us up.

LUKE SAMUEL YATES

Side effects

Disorientation, weight gain: uncommon, one in 100. Nausea: common, one in 10. Peach from space, one in 350. Smell of candles. Furry dressing gowns. When will you come and see me again? Next Tuesday depending on trains. Russians in the fish and chip shop: three fish and chips, two battered sausages, separate, two mushy peas, three cans of coke, three mini wooden forks. Curly dog once every so often. You don't like them because it's too easy to, like sunsets, forest green, me, Barcelona. The men outside church are miming something suddenly expanding and one of them catches your eye so you look away, keep walking, checking the updates, following the rules. The odds are bad but they're still odds. Coincidences all the way down the street, and a mannequin in the window looking like your young and expressionless father. 86% of this transit operator's vehicles ran on time last year. It is half past two. You can smell chips again. You are wearing your favourite anorak. The probability of rain is high for the next four hours.

GRAHAM MORT

Ischemic

There is snowfall in her voice
sifting into gullies on the mountain
resting on the sagging wires that
carry our lost wishes.

Minus-two at sixteen-hundred hours
the street untrodden   the road
laddered with tyre marks   the fields
merging   fogged by snow.

The past a blizzard   the future's
present moments measured in
fractals   in formulas of endless
mathematical permutation.

They flake from sky onto sheets
where my brother lies stroke-stunned
in the ward's infinities. I glance to
the garden remembering

fieldfare this morning   flocking
to the lawn below this window
scuffing the snow for rowan berries
with hunger's enduring rage.

Now my face   caught in the dark
glazing   her voice lowered towards
sign-off   tearful   choked by that
infarction's river silt.

Now moon's aura above the free-
hand horizon   its sac swollen with
rechargeable light   cast onto ridges
into larches where years back

I found the tonnage of a flat stone
balanced on some hidden fulcrum
saw an owl leave a branch   its white
apparition   winging it home.

CJ WAGSTAFF

Patient Positioned Supine

You appear in a moment of waking, uncanny.
Heat signature red, throbbing like an ultrasound

through an opioid fog so thick I could chew on it.
This morning you washed my hair, sat me up in bed

and fed me orange segments, face filling my whole world.
Cheeks painted pink as the walls of *The Patricia*

(our own microsystem of the Riviera).

EMILY FREEMAN

Prednisolone (or, how to love a swollen body)

I study your name
over and over, unfold your epic of side
-effects on a sheet as thin as latex, as if knowing
could change. Twice on different searches, I misspell it and
wonder if I should be putting something like you inside myself.
My tongue lumbers over the consonants; when I recount my discharge
papers to the GP, it sounds like I know almost nothing about myself. But
he has no answer to what happens next? How do we stop my body's plan to be
-come flame? And, each morning, as Venus rises too close to the sun's glare, I
feel and flex your packet, catch a glint of dawn with slow fingers and peel back a
puffed up seal. Your sterile arc rattles and waxes to finger-tip moon, now on my
tongue, bitter snowdrop. Swallow. You are still a spell I cannot pronounce; as you
dissolve, I have to accept the fate of owning this kind of body. I swell. My skin
thins and bruises when I am held by a man—I have to explain that he hasn't
hurt me. I float at the hyperreality of a meniscus, amass like a foam, and you
pull in the salt tides of my organs. I notice the feeling of my cells trying to
keep everything in, my stomach bloats to make room for more of my
-self. I cannot calm the fire of my body alone; I cannot convince
it to be less of what it feels must be. So, I picture this as
a loving act, your hands putting my red angers
out, never giving up. How tired
you must be!

DEVJANI BODEPUDI

The Strawberry Thief

After William Morris

I have fantasised
about a slit
in a bolt of fabric
I crawled through
an over-ripe strawberry
see she's sleeping or busy playing
with brown feathers left
on the floor
I slip out

Closing
the gap behind me
between seams
looking through a needlepoint
a woman with thread tangled hair
wrestles three stubborn button holes
that have lost their way-ins
through fructose screams
and sharpened fingers

caught spinning in birdsong
in Nowhere Square

don't do it
I don't
I would *never*–

stuck building high-rises
in primary colours
picking dried oats
from my areola
I seal up
escape routes

DEAN RHETORIC

Rasp(ody) in Blue

Dust   taps impatiently   on the drum skin   of the lung
chest strings   tightened   for perfect   pitch
the windpipe   works scales   in the key   of panic

the body   needs time   to adapt   and respond
the diaphragm   will join   when   it pleases
the mouth   puffed   and eager   to burst

into   not song   but still   music   listen   exhale
each rattle   lined up   each cough   in time
the air cells   conduct   the trachea   complies

orchestral   renditions   of muscles   contracting
bow fingers   tipped   tempos   kept tightly
harmonising   inside   shy octaves   of respite

blue choir   of carbon   attacking   or tuning   eight
notes   are enough   to open   the throat
one movement   one warning   one breath

SECTION VI

SAFETY CHECKS

JULIE STEVENS

Tigers

How do I cope? It's easy.
I just sink on the sofa and weep wine.
I write a thank you card to my doctor
and drench it in white vinegar. Post it
with a bloodied stamp.
I keep tigers in my wardrobe and
let them gnaw on my arms at night.
It sends them to sleep.
I fall on the shiniest floors every day
and laugh. People always walk by and
sigh. 'Come back next time,' I call out,
but they never do.
I tick every answer in my head and write
ten out of ten, because no one checks.
I tell everyone I'm fine, then quickly
phone my therapist, tell him I'm fine
and discuss it with the tigers.
They never seem to know.
When I check-in to A&E, I tell them
about the tigers, but no one seems to care.
I show them the bites on my arms
and they show me theirs.

Snails

I walk with the snails, never knowing
where my feet will land.

I can stand, sit, but what is this
if my feet refuse to move?

I walk with the snails, never knowing
if I'll crush their only shelter.

Across the lounge to the kitchen.
I should cook. Serve.

I walk with the snails, wanting to lift them,
carry them to safety.

Instead, I find another place
to collapse where no one hears.

I am a snail trying not to break.
Lift me before the day shatters.

FIONA SAMPSON

Mass

Even before I'm awake the sense of being closed in by
what? areas of shadow more than that
not areas dark patches like on tarmac after rain where we played
jumping from one to the next kids using everything to hand

these patches have a kind of muffled substance as if covered in felt
feltcovered tables and pianos in expensive libraries
or public galleries
felting to protect and conceal to block out something rare or perhaps delicate

making it pure bulk my shadows are like that pure bulk and anonymous
they move towards me speechlessly as if world and danger
are terrifying because dumb

or as if I've been deafened without realising
before I wake they've moved close to the bed like screens
for dying behind or some other humiliating & invasive procedure

VERONICA TUCKER

ROSC

We're doing compressions on a man
whose heart stopped in the Walmart parking lot
and someone notices the tattoo,

Tinkerbell bent over on his inner thigh,
wings spread, anatomically impossible.
We shouldn't laugh but we do,

three of us losing it mid-code
while the monitor shrieks
and my hands keep the rhythm going.

He lives. Walks out two days later
not knowing we saw it,
not knowing we laughed over his body

while it was still deciding
whether to come back.

Drug-Seeking

My colleague says it and I watch
the patient's face reorganize,
the small death of understanding.

He came for help. He found this.
His hand on the call button,
shaking, deciding whether to stay.

I spend twenty minutes convincing him
not to leave, that someone here
sees him as more than his urine tox.

In the parking lot I sit in my car.
I don't scream. I'm too tired to scream.
Tomorrow my colleague will say it again

about someone else and I will open
my mouth and nothing will change
and the face will reorganize anyway.

XINGYU ZHAO

Two Days At the Marie Bashir Centre

After *ode to psych wards* by Dara Goodale

Here / among the winter jacaranda / time vanishes / like an elephant's trunk / behind the steel curtains / of white rooms / sanity measured out / in bento boxes / and plastic spoons / gravity is but a trick / of dusk's bleached light / fraying yellow pages / tucked within the folds / of our palms / at night / I trace the bruised breath / of a cockatoo / against the cracked glass / of the door / I am a shrike / perched on the hinges / of the moon / a stranger's matted gown / flutters / on split bough / the lights dim / and I find a head / full of black hair / beating / beneath / my talons

VALENTINA FULGINITI

Safety Checks

some details have been altered to protect
the emotional safety of the offenders
we wouldn't want to make a dent
on the tender veneer of their shame

at age four
a slice of bread dropped on the floor
it left no crumbs as it slapped
icy kitchen tiles with the softness of a
dummy   surprise on her cheeks spread
in radiating jellyfishes of fire

at age six
her multiplications just proliferated errors
her divisions a severance of digits
her breath held quiet as the expanding wetness
of her secrets   her pearly whites a faulty abacus
that could not even tell
how many teeth were missing
already
from her mouth

by age seven she knew
comfortable numbness in the shape of her own body
and when her shaky hands had folded
every last garment in demented origamis
she folded herself inside a closet
shut her eyes shut and tasted
starbursts of pain

at age eight

at age eight

at age eight

at age eight

at age eight

at age eight

at age eight

at age eight

at age nine

she tied a shoelace against its fuzzy neck and hung

a teddy bear   from the lopsided hinges
of her childhood   she made herself judge
jury and executioner   no witness though
not a single witness   could be found

at age ten
her bedroom door flew off
and whose fault is that   whispered a shard of glass
as she began to trace its edge
on the radiating topography   of her veins

at age fifteen
she would lose herself in random twirls   of death
words appearing as themselves   ghosts coated in ink
blots on page   thoughts escaping
her hands though her hands, though shaky   her hands kept tying
words in knots   subtly undoing the fabric of her pain
they kept her tethered to the possibility   of a breath

and the brain ladies and gentlemen let's hear it for   the brain
the real MVP   the anchorman of this   surreal parade
of roaring crowds   in the oversized arena
where sequined dreams were sewn   together
I wonder how she comes up, her teachers often said
how she comes up   with such disturbing tales

at age thirty-four she heard a word

repeated   every fifteen minutes

it came with its own strange melody as she cried

for the very first time

knowing that she was at last, being kept,

that she was   at last, being watched
that she was   at last
that she was   at last
safe.

SECTION VII

FIVE YEARS IS NO TIME AT ALL

JANET DEAN

Down Graded

I would go back   to a pollen-heavy morning   a walk in gloomy shoes
an automatic turn into a side gate   a weight I was carrying from a lost place
I had moved into a sense of degradation   I admit I had done something wrong
    but not so my mother would call me shameful or wicked
or toss me out on the streets   as she imagined her father would have done to her
had she done something shameful or wicked which she never   she never did
I only smoked a cig upstairs on the bus   I didn't stab anybody
    thirsty for their blood   or even poke them in the eye with a brolly
making out I was sorry I hadn't meant to do that   (well, that one I had meant)
I didn't spot the student teacher thinking he had a duty to shop me   how did he
    make that decision? she   did he stop to think if I drop her in it
will sink and never recover that   how was he to know I had anything
could be taken away?   my pride   my elevation to the prefect class
    stripped of a badge I never collected   how was I to know
when they would be given out?   It was my skiving day   my day for a slow
walk down Summer Lane   to listen to Smoke on the Water
    to listen   to my temporary friend squealing in her boyfriend's bedroom
while I was judged to be the naughty one to   the forward one the one my
be avoided I was a terrified child   tongue misrepresented me

I go back to that still morning
    the blossom making way for tender leaves   to spread like waiting hands
and when somebody asks   are you ok? I say fine   and smile
    put away my book   I do not rush off to the toilet block   to howl
to weep   for the hole that opened up and took my future with it
    that same mother so sure of right and wrong   bewildered
        took me to a doctor   who tried all tacks at once
            the head   the heart the belly   the blood
        my satchel rattled   with those iron pills   all that Valium.

MARY MULHOLLAND

University education

In second year I returned Machiavelli's The Art
of War which my owl-faced tutor had lent me, but
he pushed me onto his desk, his wife and twin sons
went crashing to the floor, glass everywhere,
his hot breath, you're so zany, as he swooned
from my patchouli, wrestled with my kaftan,
saying a bit of summer play does no harm and he did
the marking.

After that i dyed my food black.

Two friends climbed the outer wall to my third-floor flat
came in through the window. I said they were interrupting
my essay on transgressing international waters
and could have used the stairs.

A week later A motorbiked love-blind into a bridge,
and T, a Canadian, drove up a dual carriageway
the wrong way.

My mother never let me go to funerals, so I didn't go to theirs,
just left the course to meditate on the difference between scared,
scarred and sacred, and on why stories only become stories
when facts are book-ended.

unborn

me in cream silk, pen in hand & a man, now my husband, & my parents, the vicar, a priest, all watching & waiting & i cannot write my name, this new name & what have i done & the space on the paper staring & staring at me until someone who is not me graciously steps in & writes & i'm looking at a stranger in a veil and long dress with a smile & i'm grateful & sometimes she visits & over the years she often comes until she is my go-to whenever i'm scared to be me like she's all about eve though she's not seen that yet & much later in that hospital it's she who drives there & it's she who's signing in & being led to a room where she's shedding clothes that are mine & sitting on a bed that's not mine & she, who's not me, is swallowing a pill & letting a needle enter skin that's not mine & it's not me in pastel being placed on a metal trolley & shunted into a lift then pushed down a corridor & another corridor & another & it's not me wheeled to a room with bright lights that hurt eyes that aren't mine & tears that won't stop that maybe they were once mine but now are someone else's whose temple is being stroked by a surgeon in green scrubs who might be egyptian though that's hardly relevant as it's not me he's speaking to & saying don't cry & i'm looking down & silently screaming i've changed my mind, but as if she who's not me is part of a pact which doesn't include me your cells are being scraped clear though something of you will ever stay part of me & we three will forever be an unholy trinity, a brief meeting each day to be unborn again with her in charge & you a phantom limb & me in a space where night vision's not working & dark is darker than dark.

GRAHAM CLIFFORD

Accomplice

The cleverest way to hurt someone
is to make them complicit
telling them to pull their own pants down,
that it will be worse if they don't,
so they start the show.
They pull down their pants.
He never explored 'the worse'
which may have been a more frantic flurry of hitting
with the wooden spoon
used to stir mincemeat and onions
and serve rice pudding.
By refusing to bear his arse
or to cover it with his hands
she may have gone for the fingers,
they seemed prone to breakages like mug handles
so the practical element of hurting is interesting here.
It is likely 'worse' was never fully planned
meaning this act included
the potential for free association.
'Worse'
was behind a door he would have been unwise to open.
These were lessons, in keeping with
a family with so many teachers in it.

Child Protection

If I had been my teacher
I'd have arranged for a meeting
with the Pastoral Team
who would tick boxes on the pro forma
that gets emailed to the Local Authority
who would direct us to bring you in
but not let you speak to or see your son,
to smile and quickly squeeze his wrist too hard
and use looks to threaten a collusion.
He would be ushered into another room
to play a board game
with a soft teaching assistant
whose Sugar Puffs-breath he would never forget
while I would explain to you —
holding your gaze, to see —
how it is abuse
regardless of what you think
and what the neighbours do and
what happened to you,
how the likely formal outcome
would include a non-physical chastisement order
and a further team would be convened
to decide if he was a Child in Need
or should be viewed as a Child Protection case,
at the very least this would be tracked
and everything recorded
and parenting classes would be
part of the contract. I'd finish with saying
he had better not be off sick tomorrow, knowing that
thresholds being what they are
and the crisis in recruitment what it is, and the sheer number of us
and another war and a virus and the sentinel species bowing out,
keeping an eye out
would be the only affordable strategy.
But at least I would know you know I know.

CLEMENTINE MENDELSON

Wormsong

after Song by Emily Berry

When I became a worm, it was for this reason:
the dirt sung to be eaten.
I read that I would have taste buds all over my body,
and I craved the precise care she gives to the compost heap.
To be a pink, disgusting, beautiful, wriggling thing.
Because she once told me I had snapped her in two
and I was never able to forget; I was never able to get free from it.
I wanted us to be even.
I wanted her to take up the secateurs and cut me in half,
and I wanted to live, to curl up in her palm afterwards.
Not the two halves of an ending, but of something finally over.

Five Years Is No Time at All

This is the poem in which you did not unravel.
You never learnt the smell of linoleum.
Your notebooks were not coated in a frosting of dust; your feet were not
slippered.
Friends did not speak into your absence at school,
your mother's bank statement was not half full of train fares.
Her ringtone isn't a heartbeat
stopped.
You were a loose reel of ribbon, but didn't unravel all the way —
they were able to wind you up in the outside.
You weren't a boxed fossil instead of a girl.
You are not still always split, half still-wedged in that room;
not kicked in the chest by the sweet dust of curly fries.
You never met her, and so, in your world, she never died.
You are not still wary of hospitals, and you don't go to familiar
hallway mazes in your dreams,
locked doors at every end.
You did not emerge like a foal — all flinch.
You never lost part of your life to that wormhole,
you never lost anything at all.
Every time you go to write a poem
it isn't what comes out of you,
sticky as sap.
It is not what still comes crawling out of your mouth: all flailing legs and plastic
cutlery.

HÉLÈNE DEMETRIADES

I Wonder

why the dream newt kept padding
through the cracks of my cupped fingers
last night, no longer water-bound
by feathery gills, his belly flashing
like a patrol car, why I sought
to contain the pale brown of him.

He reminds me of Sir Isaac, hatched
from an egg I brought home in a jar.
He would float in his tank, fat-eyed,
then pounce on squigglers, while
Dad lunged at me in the kitchen
my arm over my face like a wing.

Seepage

Rain from the roof leak spreads like a continent
over the sloped wall of the attic bedroom.
Downstairs, a trickle along the boxed-in girder
ruddies the ceiling. The taint looks like ooze
from a wound staining the white shirt of a Jacobite
on the battlefield. The paint blisters, plaster splits
like an overripe fruit dripping onto the parquet's
forehead. A mouse gnaws at the gut of the drain
hose; greywater seeps under the kitchen floor,
oak boards rear up from the subfloor void –
I place a bucket under the weeping.

STUART CHARLESWORTH

Adjacent to Nature and Nurture

The gaps in my learning —
            trying to get dressed
after swimming lessons, crushing
the tongue of my shoes to my toes.
Leather laces pulled to a chewed,
untied and untiable knot.

My mother would tell the professionals
who showed an interest in our welfare
that I *took things in my stride,*
I have no idea what she meant.
But to avoid certain
                        difficult lessons
I would go out in wellington boots
in summer and transform into a lizard.

It was the tail that you'd notice first,
my superextended em dash—
but my true shape remained hidden
for as long as I chose
                        to stay still.
A latent agility presupposed
by the sunlight dancing
on my perfect
black eye.

A Pernicious Gloss of Complicit

It never needed to be spoken aloud. *It —*
was invoked with smiles,
gifts of candies, sweet currencies, threats
of cruelty, to physically hurt, to let a hint slip,
be spoken with volume and breath. *Complicit —*
the word formed sharp,
crystalline, heavy and cold from the *con-*
densing fog of those insubstantial
almost-sentences, those what-might-become words
intoned by internal monologues. The narrative *chorused —*
chansoned and chanted beneath louder scripts,
where events occurred only to
others involved. Others implicated. *Illicit —*
an unwelcome loss and absence
of sound, of trust of one's self. A perversion of the *course —*
the cause of caring. An animal stink up the nose, of a something
impaired and lacking, that got on the skin and *resist-*
ed the perfume of soap
and the scolding of water from the hot tap. The *Implicat-*
ion of these cloying and *Comply-*
ing, texts was *control —*
was that they brought the shame onto themselves.

Rumours of Tunnels —

A child digs in the garden,
finds the rib bones
of a Black-Death victim.

Rumour has it,
there are plague pits
full of thrown-in corpses — rumours

of so-called sinners
bricked-up in the monastery
at the village hinterland.

The child plays in the bedroom,
hears monk-talk rising
through the floorboards:

Child, gather up those books —

bring them underground to us
we shall carry them away

to the muddy riverside.
Inspectors are traveling fast —
to investigate our ways —

trust the ferry is still moored
on the Humber. We shall fail
surely, in their spiritless exam.

This is not a solid village,
this is shifting, skitter-soil.
Do not hide your bodies here.

TRISH REEVES

What we know about the absence of light

depends who you ask, doesn't it.

My grandmother once told me of being awakened
in the night by a woman's scream—so piercing
that Grandmother ran down the hallway
in her nightgown, flung open the door
to the small balcony, and stepped
into the darkness, to stand there, the frail, wooden
balustrade at her waist, while she waited for something
more from the woman, from the emptiness
of the country road, furrowed surrounding fields
and square miles absent of any other homes
but the lairs, burrows, and webs.

It was night when she told this story.
And didn't I wonder what she thought,
knowing not to ask her
if she ever had been more afraid?

SECTION VIII

DESIRE INSIDE A YEARNING FOR THE DEEP

ITALO FERRANTE

carrie

gay terror on a home-alone friday night
nightmares of jocks pelting me with beads
bucketfuls of water-sport gunk i break
into a chuckle a sob a giggly ugly sob
if this was a thriller there'd be no fight craft
only bruised ears & real femme moans
& ghosting that feels like a manhole
penetrated by the sharpest stiletto
jesus never fails but he failed on me
my sissy voice sews up all glory holes
my forehead veins throb in tinder red
thou shalt not suffer a queer to live
my father keeps me locked in the prayer
closet closest to his private study
so i can join my hands while i hear him fuck
someone's mother in a hetero-biblical way
now the devil has come home
his camera stalks me not in the shower
because i'm not judas twunk enough
i'm not christ athletic & addicted to raw eggs
i'm no clean-shaven sexy-teary madonna
i'm a hairy side condemned to bald anal hell
& the devil wouldn't lay a finger on me

queer

i build a diorama of all the places you visit
a miniature me walks through the everywhere/
nowhere city where you last touched
the track marks on my arms

i can't live inside you
the world bursts translucent
see-through arms reach for derailed necks
my breath is smog in your eyes

i'm not queer – i'm disembodied
i turn into a leper who bleeds & screams
guttural like the tv set's squawks
ghastly like a leer of naked lust

we're all parts of a tremendous whole
i become a pig covered in brandy bruises
remember to pop these fleshy balloons
& kick my heart still

promising young woman

i don't care if you're stone-cold sober
or sprawled crucifix-style on a bench
i picture us in music video close-ups
denim-clad crotches throbbing in sync
oiled-up frames where you can see it all
don't mind the other men cheering & jeering
they just care about my body count
hey hey don't go to sleep
i can climb on your head & smother you
with my knees my manhood my one-sided kisses
you don't need all those candy-wrapper pastels
no acid wigs for that head short of testosterone
you only need those perfect blow-job lips
porno-pink & butter-fleshed
like ripe grapefruit squashed under tractors
you'll be the one crying in the morning
my friends will see you crawl out of my bedroom
& pause their pc games only to remind you
it's a question of stamina

THOMAS STEWART

Llywelyn climbs a giant

and she smelt of a summer heath, reminded me
of my sister when the sun was setting –
what is an elder sister if not a giant
one climbs from ankle to face? To look in the eye

of a giant is to see a god reflected. The giant held me
to her chest in hands the size of graveyards. A city gap-
toothed in her palms. A century of skies clouded

in her fingerprints. *Here is some knowledge from my*
experience. I imagine it is close to what Prometheus felt –
to drink something only fit for a god. If so,
let me have it. Fill me with your light.

Self-Portrait with Crown

A throatful of waves. Hurricanes locked in my eyebrows.
A mouth spilling with rockweed. Ears boxed with brine.
Barnacled bones. Tongues of inky seagrass. Pebble eyes.
Lines have already appeared, the unfinished songs of sirens.
A tooth missing its place among the crowd. I am merely an inlet.
Sometimes, the only thing to fill that blank space with is a silence.
One that might just me take me under.
Do I know this face any more than I know the ogin's secrets?
Anymore than I could look into the eye of the sea and find a reflection?

YURI LEVING

The Woman-Knife

She's a small Swiss army knife—
within her hide many secret skills
no one suspects
until she unfolds them:
a phrase pulled out like a corkscrew,
serrated edges of unpleasant conversations.

All sorts of wounds—jagged and piercing—
are laid across the skin
with a craftsman's precision,
now mingling
with memories of nightly caresses.

I have compiled a grand atlas
of the birthmarks on your body.

But more surprises await—
from her pocket, she produces
a Swiss wooden cuckoo clock.
Though it's already midnight,
the bird stays hidden.
The mechanism seems intact,
the hands keep turning,
the metal chain with pinecone weights
one crawling upward, the other down...

How much time do we have left together?
Tell me, cuckoo.

The blade,
the screwdriver,
the can opener—
she slices him into thin shavings,
wraps him in newspaper.
Keeps him safe.

SECTION IX

ON NOT SPEAKING

MAHA SALIH

A Souvenir

I stole my paperweight from Babylon.
Small I, straw-hatted, sundressed, left my mother's side;
spotted and scavenged a broken green-glazed brick,
that strained my pocket as we toured the site,
that hot day. My sandals scuffed up dust; it was hard
to see, in lumps and stubs, the city that was there.

King Nebuchadnezzar first built the city there,
that Wonder of the World that was Babylon.
Enslaved masons mixed clay and straw to shape hard-
baked bricks that built palace, gardens, temples inside
high walls, where inscribed plaques named the proud sight,
the shimmering city of green and blue glazed brick.

After it fell, villagers scavenged the glazed bricks;
built sturdy homes and barns and stables. Others,
later, reflected on the ruined site -
Don't aspire. Towers ask for trouble. *Babylon*
the Great is fallen - traumatised by urbicide
of the shimmering city now toppled and charred.

German archaeologists spotted glazed shards;
found the sound masonry of the blue-green brick
Ishtar Gate. They rebuilt it in Berlin, inside
the Pergamon: where I what's-app'd my mother:
'Remember when we walked in Babylon?
And that wasn't there? – they'd shipped it from the site.'

There's a new gate now. Saddam rebuilt the site -
dictator-bling, claiming heritage for hard-
man rule, he raised again the walls of Babylon.
Then Americans parked their tanks on ancient bricks;
levelled the ground for helipads and filled their
sandbags with crushed tiles. Kept souvenirs besides.

I kept a postcard, carefully pasted inside
an album of loudly coloured Iraqi sights
(marshes, mosques, tower blocks); sometimes forgot whether
I'd even seen them, or not, with no hard
trace of presence. But that stolen green-glazed brick
told me that once I walked in Babylon.

They prophesied skyscrapers at Babel. On
that plain there, cities began: *Let us make brick;*
sighting all the futures as the clay hardened.

After the Trade Fair

Spring morning: Tokyo, 1979;
hotel lobby. Hungover delegates,
modern young men in Western suits and ties,

groan but start already to reminisce
on contacts, prototypes, banquets, saki,
lakeside cherry blossom, the old palace.

The government minder counts his party,
goes to the desk to sign off the account.
Our man watches him turn. Gut churning, he

heads visibly to the lavatory out
the back and he's gone.   Defected.
Bags abandoned. Onwards. He walks and counts

the lefts and rights, retracing the guided
tour, heading for the UK embassy,
lakeside; appeals to be reunited

with his British wife and their family.
That's the happy ending of my father's
escape. He came to enjoy the story.

He lived his life; loved, worked, played and prospered;
never saw his birthland or his mother
again, nor heard what happened to the minder.

On Not Speaking Arabic

Medieval! And Arabic! O ghazal, I'm sold. Line
me up to wrestle again that centuries-old line.

But we broke up, me and Arabic. My sullen fist
spoilt my book scrawling clumsily across the fold line.

I learnt badly, I left, I forgot. I relinquished
a culture, and a cousinage proud of our old line.

Dad enjoyed red wine and roast pork; he loved Qur'anic
Arabic: calligraphy to me just a bold line.

Common mortality took Dad; geopolitics
Iraq. But I left the language's rippling scrolled line.

This is the ghazal of Maha, the gazelle. My name,
my last word, Dad's gift, round my neck, a twisting gold line.

RAYMOND ANTROBUS

Aboard in Dublin, Parnell Street (Formerly Great Britain Street)

I join a crowd of noise. We wave
flags of the overlooked, we block all motorised
movement with our arms and legs and voices

as a man in a white coat pushes through us
like Moses and megaphones all the right sides
to our argument. His white honest hair shines

we chant "FREE FREE", the word becoming a foot
against the guarded door
of courts and parliaments, "FREE FREE"

we blast our jaws of resistance.
Then a smaller crowd counters, waves
an ironic St George flag, the cross

of my own nation. Their sign reads
"All problems began with the English"
Another sign reads, "Bomb The English"

Of course I feel the sun lower
its eyes on me as I move
to the side, become a fissure

in what was once united, letting a new meaning
divide me
from the crowd I joined. What is this

instinct to go quiet? To show allegiance
to silence. Perhaps my silence
is all I can control. I cannot control

the reading of *English,*
the sound it makes, cannot free it
from the violence of its own palace.

SECTION X
WITHIN RINGROADS

STEVEN GREEN

Whoa There White Lightning

I'm watching your foot batter the side of a bin
in perpetual motion, the twang volleyed
through the Queensway tunnel
like a row of archers firing arrows into its mouth
as we wait for the 50 to your friend's house.
I had to ask if it hurt but you said no
because you knew how to kick properly.
Your hormones frenzied with two litres
of White Lightning sloshing in your guts,
your concentrated brow keeping the pain dull.
I thought about your foot throbbing
in the sausage casing of your sock,
the muscles humming through brute force,
tendons taut against the bone,
stuffed inside your fat skate shoes -
soles like melting Soleros. I knew better
than to ask where your girlfriend was.
Why her absence had led to this medieval beatdown
of city property. We were meant to drink a beer,
smoke something, pick a moment
to find funny before we knocked out
in a tiled room of peeling posters
and milk carton bongs. I wonder
if you went to sleep dreaming about her
and what was wrong with you,
or if you finally dreamt that there was nothing
wrong with you at all.

KATHERINE HORREX

Within Ringroads

snailskin tarmac, a sky of eaves. Beery rivers teeming with beer
coloured trout. Orange water margins halfway up your calves
and chlorinated mud. Bale-sized dogs in punnet-sized backyards.
Grave-robber ginnels. Chipped mills toothy as broken crockery.
The badger keystones of a Tudor hall, half covered in scaffolding.
Plum splat and toffee glazed evenings. The crystalline burning
of sugar in molars. Sinkwater mornings brackish with grounds.
Regional weeklies, their headlines re. women who each went out
like bulbs on dimmer switches. Of bleary gusts

and bleary rhythmic twinkling. Tracing a toenail's gloss ridges
in front of an electric fire now the closest thing to toasted
marshmallows. More than half the seasons our pores wince
like stars. Angry men in doctored cars always on the road's
wrong side. Of Love Island falsies endorsed by Kardashians.
Of Chicken Cottage and Chicken Lodge and one day Chicken
Outhouse. Another day, simply Chicken. The cursive pout
of the purple font on a tanning salon's discount vouchers.
Of deciduous currency. Wooden architraving
which flakes like so much gold leaf.

ALISON TANIK

A year in Ireland

But the sheep swimming in the tidal meadows are worrying me/and the children are doing the loop again to Lomanagh Bridge, muddy shoes piled by the fire/and Teddy O'Neill is at the door with his arms in amber, kitchen-table knots/and the house on the way to the standing stone has sheep at its windows, even upstairs/ and the dead foxes at Murphy's farm, hanging black-red on the gate posts, shout Teddy's name to me/and there are more fossils than jam jars on the kitchen shelves now/and when I do the Monday clean, whiskey-glass shards are coming out from under the sofa/and the Famine house each day becomes less, leaning into the hill like a drunk/and in the doctor's parlour, Mrs O'Sullivan asks me why I am there/and the peat behind the house is laid out like fresh-cut body bags/and the rain//

SECTION XI

THE LAKE INTO WHICH ALL THINGS ARE SUNK

GEORGIA HILTON

Sometimes I fear I am the lake

into which all things are sunk. The keys
to the old house, the useless degree
certificate. The duffel bag containing
all your old CDs. The fake IDs.
Your entire relationship history,
which, although short,
goes hard on brutality.

That Pulp Fiction haircut,
your crush on Eddie Vedder,
your attachment to sex as
the white flag of surrender.
The bruises down the left side
of your body as you exited
the car abruptly. The rock that
threatened to smash your head in.

Too large to be a skimming stone,
but look, when it hits the water,
it makes impressive expanding rings
before it settles on the lakebed,
goes incognito. Impossible
at those murky depths to tell one
guilty stone from the rest of them.

ALLISON ZHANG

Etymology of a Shrug

The neurologist says it's non-progressive.
Which feels generous.

At breakfast, my grandfather lifts a spoon,
stalls midair, points at the cereal.
Calls it *sky*.

I nod. Sure.
Everything falls eventually.

He once told me
the first English word he learned was *wait*.
It was also the last thing he said to me.
Maybe that's coincidence.
Or a loop.

At the DMV, he gave his birth year as 1857.
Said his job was "still becoming."
The clerk didn't blink. Typed it in.

When he was nine,
a soldier asked his name.
He said it. They laughed.
That was the year he stopped answering.

The MRI lit his brain like a city after rain.
One hemisphere fogged.
The other—
a grocery list in half-light:
eggs.
mercy.
something that starts with *forgive*.

Yesterday, he pointed at a crow and said *God*.
Then laughed,
like the punchline arrived late.
I wrote it down anyway.

At the root, *shrug* means "to writhe."
Which might explain how I love—
and why I wear jackets
with sleeves past my knuckles.

Grass Mirror

for the ones who swore they never lied

Uncle bites through his orange and begins—
his teeth bright with pulp,
hands slick from rind,
juice tracking the knuckles.

He tells us about the mirror
buried beneath the sugar peas,
how roots wrap around it
when someone tells
what the world refuses.

My cousin scrapes a basin
into the field with her heel,
daring me to break something.

So I do—
three twists of the tongue
that scald like wire:
I didn't take it.
I didn't close the gate behind you.
I didn't wish for the sting.

The air strains.
Something shifts beneath the crust—
a dull film, warped and veined,
drawn across the mud
as if the soil had grown an eye.

She bolts.
I kneel.

It shows a girl with my arms.
Her gaze isn't mine.

Later, Uncle rinses our palms
in a chipped basin behind the shed.

He says nothing,
but his grip lingers.
I know he's seen it too.

That night, I wake to the sound

of something digging toward me.

Fingers.
Searching.

Self-Portrait With Scissors

I build a girl from butcher paper.
She arrives folded. The creases stay.

Her arms outstretch mine.
She touches the ceiling
like it owed her nothing.

I give her a red mouth—
not a smile. Just red.
I say:
stand like no one ever taught you waiting.

She stands.
She waits.

I cut her new clothes:
a denim jacket, a bias-cut dress,
a pocket for something she'll misplace
but swear she never needed.

She asks
if I've ever loved
without disappearing
into someone else's outline.

I say:
once, I stepped away from the glass
and it filled with everything I wasn't.

She folds herself into a chair.
I fold the chair flat.

You're cruel, she says.
No, I tell her—just done
being the sketch
instead of the body.

Later, I sketch a door with no handle.
She walks through.
Leaves the paper behind,
but keeps the blade.

SECTION XII

THE IMAGE HAS FAILED US

SUE HUBBARD

Julia 1988-9

After Frank Auerbach

He rubs the wet skin raw again,
erases strings and rope-knots

of glutinous paint,
those near approximations

of meaning flawed as words,
with the wrong end of his brush,

erases the thick *Flake White,*
Indian Red and *Yellow Ochre*

on the collapsing canvas
with a blue rag

in search of that edge
between reality and essence.

Though he's known her bare flesh
beneath the rose-strewn

eiderdown, here, before
the smoking studio stove

he builds a palimpsest of paint
to catch, not so much

the angle of her nose,
knee or breast, but her quintessence,

for to become visible
is to be vulnerable,

a way, amid our human terror,
of simply being here.

SUZI FEAY

Crystal Skull

To worship you must climb the stair
Where head-high on a pedestal
Gleams the grimacing artefact
Pulsating with a glassy glare
A premonition fateful, clear.
The label states: vague origin
Occult purpose, Mexican.
Later devices spoiled the tale:
No alien craft, uncanny skill
Ancient transmitter or power store
But detailed by a dentist's drill
And centuries younger than its lore.

I searched among the capes
And cups and cabinets. No luck.
No longer on display, the fake's
Been shelved. We shouldn't shy
From our embarrassments –
Empty sockets and a loveless smile
I thought I'd seen right through.
I was so easy to beguile
With antipasti in Primrose Hill
Taking every boast for true:
'You will never fathom me...'
Unwilling still to comprehend
With provenance in gem or friend
The simplest answer will amend.

Unpick

Where to begin? The gifted teapot
Pushed where I don't have to look at it
Designer cartons, ribboned, stiff
Dropped in the recycling with receipts
I make a sweep of any lingering stuff.

The patterned plate, the slogan cup
I'll have to keep. Can't get rid
Of couch or dining chair despite
The surly shadow that they summon up
Pillows slouch suggestive on the bed.

Places are hardest; cafes whose lintels
I flinch past squinting at a vacant stool
Pubs where a dark vortex still
Flickers by the pumps. A leather chair
Bears sagging witness in a corner bar.

Then the imaginary of otherwhere:
Red plush at the Opera House
A cap forgotten in a restaurant –
Distracted much by legs and hair?
I wouldn't know. I wasn't there.

A buzzing doorway in a sombre square
A blitz of messages that bind;
Perfidious sheen of begging eyes
Then promises all rolled up like ties
Folded in secret pockets of the mind.

LAURA THEIS

Tombstone Emoji

I did not go to the school
reunion but I did join
the group chat in order to lurk for years
in a surreal space where awkward old in-jokes
jostle against absurd announcements:
Miss Gesing died funeral this Friday at six tombstone emoji
followed by a whole
paragraph about Miss Gesing's bereaved
litter of cats looking for immediate adoption
(temptingly, they come with their own
endowment)
the most liked post is
a selfie of some bearded guy I don't recognise
next to old Mr Radnoti looking exactly
the same as he did twenty years ago
and although no part of me is tempted to type
woah drop the skincare routine Radnoti
I do not leave the chat or mute the group
since thanks to whichever teacher it was who made us read the elegies I like to
be reminded sometimes that *beauty is nothing but the beginning of terror which we*
are barely able to endure

SECTION XIII

I'M HERE, LOVE, THE CAVALRY ARE ON THEIR WAY

BETTY POWDRILL

Tempered

i text
are you there?
adrenaline thumping through
my chest

yes my love –
are you ok? x

i try to explain

oh honey,

i try again

it would explain why the
positive lines were
so faint

you hold me in that moment
like a glass bowl
calm, robust hands
with fingerprints pressed hard

how could i ever possibly
shatter?

Blackout

they tell me there was a total eclipse
the moon doing its best to upstage the sun
edging on from the wings

slowly

gently

thenallatonce

and everybody called it
a spectacle

when my darkness enters
casting shadows where i stand

i just hope everyone is as forgiving

C. E. REGAN

I think I love you, four hours thirty-six minutes into Max Richter's Sleep

Floorboards creak under the cellist's chair
as she breathes in and out. I think of you
holographic behind the structures of sound, between
C-sharp major pulled over fresh rosin on horsehair & tiny squeals
the musician's fingertips make pressing white on strings.
Crows scratch on the roof of morning,
holding, then losing their footsteps, like rain.
My reflection wobbles on the shine of my coffee
I drink until I see you, in the body of my swallow sound

You find me kneeling, counting my affects. Do I have enough heart
touch, humour, blood, sleep, nerves for both of us?
You lie down on the kitchen floor, I count you, before I
make a cut under your belly button one inch wide and deep
I choose an old, silky scar over a vein
open it   drip   drip   drip   drip   drip
into you all the red and universe I can give.

You turn pink, your cheeks hope-plump and I want
to squeeze you until you reflect light
I want your thank yous and your black star
on their knees with my small stoic spark.

DANIEL ROY CONNELLY

Public Service Announcement #35

... and for the sake of your mental health don't forget
to let the world carry on without you a while.
You owe it to yourself to switch off now and again.
Permit the trees to shake their angry branches,
the grass to waver on the edge of total collapse,
the air to recycle itself into something even worse.
They couldn't care less about your chuntering. Let go.
Even when the granite sky bears down its brunt on your pain,
let go. They are elements. They are not the whole of anything.

Consider the opposites of what you disdain.
List them as above, locate and pass through them,
or rather they through you, give every
flowing image a thought and place
them in your distinguished repertoire,
ready for recall at a moment's notice.
What counts most is the deep desire for change.
We are ice massed in a hanging glacier.
All it takes is the courage to melt.

JUDITH WOZNIAK

Broken

In the cave of your garage you store odd bits
of wood, wingnuts, jars of nails, just in case
they come in useful. You mend broken toys

with matchstick splints, wicks of cotton
dipped in glue. Last summer you helped
our grandson make a boat to sail on the canal.

It was your hands I first noticed, musicians' hands
that played the violin in Luton Schools Orchestra,
the rickety piano in your front room, cold as a tomb.

Hands that thread fine tubes into premature babies
in incubators under hot lights. The same hands
gently holding open my airway after the accident.

I'm here love
the cavalry are on their way.

MAX WALLIS

Shopping List

after Simon Armitage

I can walk in wherever I want and buy whatever I want and I do, sometimes.
But sometimes I just go out in search of a new heart, and get cucumbers.

Or do I mean pickles? Or do I mean the sharp green afterlife
of something once clean? Everything burdened by a barcode, useful and useless,

don't they know I have been locked up for years, but the cage is just transparent?
Maybe I'm looking for a refurbished heart without a warranty, though they say there's one

and it turns out to be invalid, or a heart someone brought back
because it was the wrong size, or one marked down because a heart attack stopped it dead.

I think I need broken eggs. So I can blame someone else for the cracking.
Milk, but not the blue one, and I'll slot it in the fridge next to the three dirty sentinels

months past their expiry, cursed with whey, the moulded pot,
all of them things I could change but can't, like bread with seeds in

to suggest I am still in progress, now a colony of my own doing.
Butter, salted, maybe, because unsalted is a lie told by people with calm kitchens,

gemstone butter, yes, gemstone butter, the kind kept cold in a palace fridge,
Fabergé mittens, one for each hand I no longer know what to do with,

a bag for life that understands this is optimistic, a bag for the past,
a bag for the version of me who could walk into a shop and only need onions.

I can steal the heart if needed, not from a person, from a saint,
or from a butcher, from the chilled aisle, from the diagram on the wall,

from a Valentine's display already half-price, because it's past February.
I need cling film for the parts of me still open,

tin foil for my little conspiracy of grief, kitchen roll, industrial kitchen roll,
the kind that absorbs blood, rain, milk, panic, whatever I spill next,

bin bags, stronger bin bags, council-strength bin bags, black enough
to make an ending look tidy, washing powder for clothes I have already ruined,

fabric softener because I would like to be less proof of what it is to be me,
cat food, the expensive kind, so someone in this house eats like they are loved,

batteries, AA, AAA, whatever fits the small dead things, a torch, a second torch
for when the first one becomes metaphor, one clean knife, one blunt knife,

one knife that remembers bread and not the other things,
receipt paper long enough to prove I was here and a loyalty card for disloyalty,

a self-checkout that does not say unexpected item when I stand on the scales,
grapes, green grapes, seedless, obviously, I have enough small hard futures

lodged in me already. A melon for carrying home like a head. Cabbage
to carry like it's going to become my baby.

Tea bags, coffee, decaf coffee for the person I keep promising to become,
sugar, no sugar, no, sugar, and matches and candles and flowers,

not funeral flowers, not apology flowers, just flowers or a plant
that I am allowed to neglect,

a new mouth, a mouth that says thank you and means no,
a mouth that can ask where the hearts are kept,

washing-up liquid, the pink one, or the green one,
no, the one that makes my hands smell briefly innocent,

rice, pasta, lentils, things people buy when they believe in next week,
a new heart. I know I said that, but put it down again, put it down in capitals,

NEW HEART

organic if possible, ethically sourced, locally produced, not too dear, not too proud,
not one of those hearts that bruises if you look at it,

not one of those hearts that thinks love is a form of weather,
not one of those hearts that keeps returning to the scene,

a heart with instructions,
a heart with a helpline,

a heart I can assemble myself with the little Allen key provided,
a heart that comes flat-packed and does not mind my floor,

a heart that fits through the door of my life,
and a cucumber,

and pickles,
and eggs,

and butter,
and milk,

and bread,
and cat food,

and bin bags,
I mean honestly,

just everything
and somewhere to put it.

How to Make Friends

Begin with a phone. It doesn't matter which.
Blue-white pixels are a form of proximity.

Reply within a reasonable timeframe.
Use: mate, you okay? x.

Watch how quickly love multiplies.
Be cautious, but allow the swarm of names

and notifications, small proofs. You are not
without people. In person, keep it light.

Work will cover most of it when your hands
start to jitter with too much outside.

When the room turns cold, do not panic.
Check your phone again.

It should be full by now. No need for low-battery mode
even if you need that yourself.

Physicality can look like friendship.
But sex is rarely more than oxytocin.

Practise carrying yourself.
Say I'm fine until it sounds unremarkable.

Later you will know when to say:
I'm really not.

At home, use the air as stage.
Cats are a good audience.

So is the coffee machine.
They will stay. Until they don't.

Now stand in the centre of it:
this crowd and this quiet,

and try to tell the difference.

CONTRIBUTORS

SECTION I – WHAT DO WE NEED BUT A BIT OF HOPE?

Aaron Kent is a working-class writer who runs Broken Sleep Books. His work appears in The Poetry Review, Poetry London, and The Rialto. Author of The Working Classic and Angels the Size of Houses, he was awarded Wellbeing Champion 2025 for his work advocating for mental health and stroke survivors.

Katie Hale is a Cumbrian novelist and poet. She won a Northern Debut Award for her poetry collection, White Ghosts, and is the author of two novels: The Edge of Solitude and My Name is Monster. She is a former MacDowell Fellow, and also mentors young writers through Writing Squad.

Hollie McNish is a poet and author based between Scotland and England. She was the first poet to record at Abbey Road Studios and won the Ted Hughes Award for Nobody Told Me, her poetic parenting memoir. Her collections include Papers, Cherry Pie, Plum, Slug, Lobster and Virgin, with work translated into French and Spanish.

Oliver James Lomax is a poet, educator, and trustee of the Working-Class Movement Library in Salford. He passionately believes in cultural equality and the power of the arts to enable everyone in society to have a voice.

Peter Archer started writing as a reviewer for the New Musical Express. His poetry has been published in many magazines such as Magma, The Moth and The Interpreter's House. He is currently completing a comic sci-fi novel, and works in a University Library.

Meleri Davies is a poet, writer and community worker from Dyffryn Ogwen. Her work appears in Poetry Wales, Modron Magazine, Ffosfforws and Afonydd (Arachne Press). Her first collection of poetry Rhuo ei distawrwydd hi (Cyhoeddiadau'r Stamp; 2024) won the Wales Book of the Year 2025 award for Welsh-language poetry.

Rhys Owain Williams is from Swansea, Wales. His work has been published in magazines and anthologies, and read at events, festivals and on national television. Rhys edits The Crunch multimedia poetry magazine, and is a Hay Festival Writer at Work. His first collection, That Lone Ship, is available from Parthian.

Penny Sharman has an MA in Creative Writing from Edge Hill University.
She has had poems published in The North, Finished Creatures, Orbis & Mslexia & Candlestick Press. Her books are available from her website: pennysharman.co.uk Penny is editor of OWP poetry magazine.

Robert Hamberger has been shortlisted and highly commended for Forward prizes. His fourth collection Blue Wallpaper (Waterloo Press) was shortlisted for the 2020 Polari Prize. His latest books are the memoir A Length of Road (John Murray, 2021) and the poetry collection Nude Against A Rock (Waterloo Press, 2024).

Rosie Jackson lives in Devon. In 2025 she won the Red Shed competition, was Highly Commended in Kathryn Bevis, and in 2022 was Commended in the National. Publications include Love Leans over the Table, Two Girls and a Beehive: Poems about Stanley Spencer and The Glass Mother: A Memoir.

www.rosiejackson.org.uk

Rachel Burns has been published in literary magazines including The Rialto, Magma, Atrium, and The Friday Poem. She came second in the Disabled Poets Prize 2024. Her first poetry collection, My Last Address, Horses, Horses, Horses, will be published in 2026 by Broken Sleep Books.

Helen Mort is an award-winning poet and author based in Sheffield. Her poetry collections include Division Street, No Map Could Show Them and The Illustrated Woman, shortlisted for the Forward Prize. She has also written the novel Black Car Burning, the short story collection Exire, and the non-fiction book A Line Above The Sky. She is a Fellow of the Royal Society of Literature and Senior Lecturer at Manchester Metropolitan University.

SECTION II – AN ANTHROPOLOGY OF GRIEF

Catherine Redford started writing poetry after being widowed at 35. Her work has appeared in Magma, Under the Radar, Propel and Ink Sweat & Tears. She is an editor at Dust Poetry, a Writing West Midlands Room 204 writer and a Nine Arches Press Dynamo Poet. Her debut collection is The Way the Water Held Me.

Gemma Strang is a poet living in Folkestone, Kent. Her poems have been published in Magma and Acumen. She was Highly Commended in the Nine Arches Press 'Primers' competition in 2025.

Nicky Kippax is a poet from Yorkshire. She's a Northern Writers' Award winner and her work can be found most recently in The Rialto, Oxford Poetry, The London Magazine and PN Review. Nicky co-hosts Rise Up! - a celebration of poetry in Acomb, York.

Sally Read is the award-winning author of four poetry collections and editor of 100 Great Catholic Poems. Her poetry has been recorded for the UK's Poetry Archive and published in The Times Literary Supplement, The Picador Book of Love Poems and Forward's Poems of the Decade. Her memoirs include Night's Bright Darkness and The Mary Pages. Originally a psychiatric nurse, she now lives in Rome.

Clare Best's most recent publications are her third full collection of poetry Beyond the Gate (Worple Press 2023) and a lyric essay in BMJ Medical Humanities (April 2026) which considers representations of child sexual abuse in the arts. Her collaborative audio-documentary Blackout will be premiered at Bloomsbury Festival in October 2026. Clare is an Associate Lecturer with The Open University and a Tutor for The Arvon Foundation. She lives in Suffolk, England.

Stephen Boyce is the author of three poetry collections, Desire Lines (Arrowhead 2010), The Sisyphus Dog (Worple 2014) and The Blue Tree (Indigo Dreams 2019) and three pamphlets. He is co-founder of Winchester Poetry Festival and lives in north Dorset. stephenboycepoetry.com

Daragh Byrne is a Sydney-based Irish poet. His work has appeared in Poetry Wales, Poetry Birmingham Literary Review, Southword, Banshee and elsewhere. He has been shortlisted in the Patrick Kavanagh award and the Poetry London competitions (pamphlet/single poem) He is co-editor of The Marrow, a journal of international poetry.

Blake Morrison is a poet, novelist and journalist. His non-fiction books include And When Did You Last See Your Father? (1993), which won the J. R. Ackerley Prize. His poetry includes the collections Dark Glasses, winner of the Somerset Maugham Award, and Shingle Street. He is a regular literary critic for the Guardian and the London Review of Books.

Dr Anna Percy, a bisexual poet with bipolar disorder, completed her groundbreaking thesis at MMU: Bipolar Magpie: a 21st Century Embodied Eco-Feminist Poetics, focused on mad studies and eco-poetry. She has three collections with Flapjack Press and co-founded Stirred Poetry. Her work blends performance, experimental poetics, feminism, and the natural world, shaped by two decades of community teaching and a commitment to redefining what it means to be a mad-identified scholar. She is Contributing Editor at The Aftershock Review.

SECTION III – THE REAR BEDROOM

Abeer Ameer's poems have appeared widely in journals including The Rialto, Magma, The Poetry Review and Poetry Wales. Her debut poetry collection, Inhale/Exile (Seren) was shortlisted for Wales Book of the Year 2022. Her poem, at least, is shortlisted for Best Single Poem for the Forward Prize 2024-2025.

Özge Lena is a worldwide published poet who appears in numerous magazines as well as international anthologies across continents. Her poetry earned Pushcart Prize and Best of the Net nominations and was shortlisted for Oxford Brookes, Plough Poetry Prize, and Black Cat Poetry Press Nature Prize.

SECTION IV – THE HAPPINESS BUSINESS

Adrian Slatcher is a Manchester based writer. He has published poetry and fiction widely including most recently a book of six short stories "Loners" (Confingo Publishing, 2024).

Benedicta Norell is the author of Terrible Mother, published by Black Cat Poetry Press. The second print run is available now. Her poems appear in magazines, podcasts and anthologies, including Dust Poetry, Poetry Worth Hearing and To Lay Sun into a Forest from Sídhe Press. Website benedictanorell.com / Instagram @benedictanorell

Dan O'Brien is a poet, playwright, and nonfiction writer who has published collections of poetry in the US and in the UK, including the Fenton Aldeburgh Prize-winning War Reporter. His latest collections are Survivor's Notebook (Acre Books) and Flying on Easter (Poetry London Editions). O'Brien lives in Los Angeles.

Tom Branfoot is a poet and critic from Bradford, and the writer-in-residence at Manchester Cathedral. He won a Northern Writers' Award in 2024 and the New Poets Prize 2022. He organises the poetry reading series More Song in Bradford. Tom is the author of This Is Not an Epiphany (Smith|Doorstop) and boar (Broken Sleep Books), both published in 2023. His debut collection Volatile is forthcoming with the87press.

SECTION V – WHAT ELSE IS A BODY FOR?

Elizabeth Eger is a poet. She is currently working on a pamphlet, Deep Brain Stimulation, which addresses the experience of brain surgery for Early-onset Parkinson's disease.

Hilary Hares' poems appear widely online and in print. She has also achieved success in various competitions. She has an MA in Poetry from Manchester Metropolitan University and her three pamphlets are available through: www.hilaryhares.com. Her debut collection, Tilting at Windmills, will be published by Poetry Space in summer 2026.

Angi Holden is a retired lecturer, whose poetry and prose explore differing perspectives of relationships and identity, within a broader context of memory. Most recently she has worked on ekphrastic and collaborative projects inspired by the intersections between writing and arts, crafts & photography.

Maura Dooley lives in London. She has published several collections with Bloodaxe Books, most recently Five Fifty-Five.

Jessica Mookherjee is a British poet of Bengali heritage, is widely published in UK and is the author of 4 collections, three with Nine Arches Press and one with Broken Sleep Books (Desire Lines). Jessica's book Tigress was shortlisted for the Ledbury prize and she was twice highly commended in the Forward Prize. Her fourth collection with Nine Arches Press is out in November 2026 called "The Universe is an Animal".

Katrina Moinet's debut pamphlet Portrait of a Young Girl Falling shortlisted for Wales Book of the Year 2025. Katrina is poetry editor for Raw Lit, editor at (an)arferol | (un)common magazine and hosts Versify open mic night. Their work is widely published, including Poetry Wales, iamb, Mslexia Best Women's Short Fiction and Ffosfforws, and has won or placed in several writing competitions. Their debut novel is in development with Seren Books.

Luke Samuel Yates is a poet and sociologist based in Manchester. His first collection, Dynamo (2023) was a winner of the Poetry Business International Book and Pamphlet Prize. He has published two poetry pamphlets: The Pair of Scissors that Could Cut Anything, and The Flemish Primitives.

Graham Mort is emeritus professor of Creative Writing at Lancaster University. He lives in North Yorkshire and has published ten collections of poetry and three volumes of short fiction. Graham is currently working on a new collection of poems, 'Rivers Joining' and a new book of stories, 'Émigrés'.

CJ Wagstaff is a poet, musician, and nonfiction writer from South Wales. He is a recipient of the 2024 Nigel Jenkins Award and is currently completing a PhD in creative non-fiction. His work appears in Propel Magazine, Poetry Wales, and Buzz Magazine.

Emily Freeman is a Nottingham-based poet. She runs workshops with The Paper School at the National Poetry Library in London. A previous finalist in the Mslexia Poetry Competition, her work often explores language failure, intimacy, illness, and the body. She has an upcoming poem featured in issue 7 of Sick Magazine.

Devjani Bodepudi is a British Indian poet. Her work has appeared in Spelt Poetry Magazine, Wasifiri and Dust, amongst others. Her debut poetry pamphlet won a Saboteur Award in 2023. Devjani is currently pursuing a PhD at Manchester Metropolitan University, examining transformation and grief in folk tales and Indic Mythic traditions.

Dean Rhetoric is a poet living in Manchester. His debut full-length collection, Foundry Songs, is available from Broken Sleep Books and was Highly Commended for the Forward Prize.

SECTION VI – SAFETY CHECKS

Julie Stevens writes poems that cover many themes but often engages with the problems of disability. She is widely published in places such as anthologies from Macmillan and OUP, Acumen, Broken Sleep Books, Indigo Dreams Publishing and on Ink Sweat & Tears. She has five published pamphlets. Website: www.jumpingjulespoetry.com.

Fiona Sampson is a New York Times bestseller writer who has been published in 38 languages.
Her most recent poetry collection, Come Down (Corsair, 2021) received the European Lyric Atlas

prize, Naim Frasheri laureateship and Wales Poetry Book of the Year.

Veronica Tucker is an emergency medicine and addiction medicine physician. A Pushcart Prize nominee, her work appears in ONE ART, The Berlin Literary Review, and Rust & Moth. She lives in New Hampshire. Her debut chapbook is forthcoming. @veronicatuckerwrites

Xingyu Zhao is reading literature on the sunny island of Singapore. His work has appeared in Portside Review, Cordite Poetry Review, ONE ART, Funicular Magazine, Aethlon, and elsewhere.

Valentina Fulginiti is an alumna of the universities of Toronto and Bologna and currently a Senior Lecturer at Cornell University. Her debut novel won the premio Bianciardi inediti in 2024 and is forthcoming in Italy. Her poems are forthcoming in Merion West and The Sacramento Literary Review.

SECTION VII – FIVE YEARS IS NO TIME AT ALL

Janet Dean's poetry is published in magazines and competition anthologies in print and online. Most recently she has been Highly Commended for the Bridport and Manchester Cathedral Prizes , and commended in the Poetry Society Stanza Competition.

Mary Mulholland is published in many magazines, such as, recently, The Marrow International, Eche, 14 Magazine, Anthropocene, and has been mentioned in many competitions, such as third in Write Out Loud, HC in Ware.

Graham Clifford is a British author of five collections of poetry. His work can be found on the Poetry Archive, and is anthologised by publishers including Faber, Against the Grain and Broken Sleep Books. Most recently, his work has been included in the Manchester Review, Finished Creatures and BerlinLit.

Clementine Mendelson (she/her) is a poet whose work explores memory, trauma, and the body — specifically teeth and bones. She grew up in London, and recently graduated from the University of Birmingham with an English Literature degree. Her poetry has been published or is upcoming in Willows Wept Review, Antlers, HNDL Magazine, and Prosetrics. Find her on Instagram @ clementineiswriting.

Hélène Demetriades' debut collection 'The Plumb Line' was published by Hedgehog Press in 2022. She won the Silver Wyvern, 2022, and was longlisted in The National, 2023. She came equal 4th in the Kent & Sussex Poetry Competition, 2025. Her poems have recently appeared in Magma and The Interpreter's House.

Poet and nurse Stuart Charlesworth, works in Mental Health services. They have been shortlisted in the Live Canon poetry competition and the Rialto pamphlet competition. They were commended in the 2018 Brittle Star competition and the 2021 Hippocrates prize. Stuart has a creative writing MA and helps run Café Writers.

Trish Reeves has received fellowships from the National Endowment for the Arts, Yaddo, Sarah Lawrence College, and Kansas Arts Commission. For 21 years Reeves taught English and Creative Writing at Haskell Indian Nations University, and led Changing Lives Through Literature for Johnson County Corrections. She is a Humanities Kansas Scholar.

SECTION VIII – DESIRE INSIDE A YEARNING FOR THE DEEP

Italo Ferrante is a queer poet and video artist who is currently working on a creative PhD on trauma theory at Manchester Metropolitan University. To date, Italo's work has been accepted for publication by Poetry Salzburg, Impossible Archetype, Cardiff Review, Stone of Madness, bath magg, Lighthouse, and BODY.

Thomas Stewart was born in Cardiff and lives in Edinburgh. He is the author of Real Boys (Polygon, 2024) and two pamphlets, Based on a True Story (fourteen poems, 2022) and empire of dirt (Red Squirrel Press, 2019).

Yuri Leving teaches contemporary Russian literature and film at Princeton University. His books and edited collections include Nabokov in Motion (2022), A Revolution of the Visible (2018), Marketing Literature and Posthumous Legacies (2013), Lolita: The Story of a Cover Girl (2013), Anatomy of a Short Story (2012), and Keys to The Gift (2011). He has also directed and produced three documentaries on Joseph Brodsky, Vladimir Nabokov, and, most recently, Akhmatova's Orphans: Disassembly (2024). A bilingual poet, Leving has published primarily in Russian; however, after the full-scale invasion of Ukraine, he began writing in English. He was named a Guggenheim Fellow in 2023.

SECTION IX – ON NOT SPEAKING

Maha Salih is a medievalist who lives and works in London. She has previously published poems in Poetry London, Amethyst Review, South and The Frogmore Papers.

Raymond Antrobus is the author of four poetry collections — To Sweeten Bitter, The Perseverance, All The Names Given, and Signs, Music — as well as two children's books: Can Bears Ski? and Terrible Horses. In 2025 he published the memoir The Quiet Ear: An Investigation of Missing Sound.

SECTION X – WITHIN RINGROADS

Steven Green is a London-based poet from Birmingham. His work has appeared in Bruiser, Clarion, Gold Dust and in anthologies from Broken Sleep Books and Morocco Bound. He is working on his debut pamphlet and is currently studying a Masters in Creative Writing at Goldsmiths.

Katherine Horrex is a poet published by Carcanet. Her collection Growlery was a finalist in the Seamus Heaney First Collection Prize and commended in the Forward Prizes.

Alison Tanik is a poet/performer who came to writing in her mid-50s. She has an MA in poetry from MMU. Her work has appeared in anthologies and literary magazines and has won prizes including the DPF East Midlands Prize 2024 and the River Heron Poetry Review Prize 2025.

SECTION XI – THE LAKE INTO WHICH ALL THINGS ARE SUNK

Georgia Hilton is an Irish poet living in Winchester. She is the author of two books of poetry (Dempsey and Windle) and co-author of a collaborative pamphlet (Nine Pens Press). Along with folk group !nverse she recently created and performed an original spoken word show about the Swing Riots.

Allison Zhang is a writer and editor based in Los Angeles. An immigrant and bilingual speaker of English and Mandarin, she writes about language and memory. Her work appears or is forthcoming in Pithead Chapel, Midway Journal, Vagabond City Lit, SWWIM Every Day, and Stone Circle Review, among others.

SECTION XII – THE IMAGE HAS FAILED US

Sue Hubbard is an award-winning poet, novelist and art critic. She has published five collections of poetry, a book of short stories and four acclaimed novels. She has an MA in Creative Writing from UEA.

Suzi Feay was literary editor of the Independent on Sunday for 11 years, and subsequently its poetry reviewer. She has published poems in The London Magazine, Magma, Poetry Review and Poetry Scotland, and has read at various literary festivals, the Courtauld gallery in London, and the South Bank. She is a member of the Critics Circle and the Authors Club, and a regular judge of the annual Polari Prize. She is Contributing Editor at The Aftershock Review.

Laura Theis's work appears in Poetry, Oxford Poetry, The Irish Times, etc.
Accolades include the Caterpillar Prize, Alpine Fellowship, Oxford-Brookes-Poetry-Prize, Arthur-Welton-Award. Her most recent collections are Introduction To Cloud Care (Broken Sleep) and Poems from a Witch's Pocket (Emma Press).

SECTION XIII – I'M HERE, LOVE, THE CAVALRY ARE ON THEIR WAY

Betty Powdrill is a poet based in Yorkshire, England. A sucker for noticing tiny moments and buying more notebooks than she'll ever be able to fill, she drafts in pencil – messy and urgent – before pressing her words into permanence on her vintage typewriter.

C. E. Regan is from Ireland. She was part of the Freedom to Write Project 2025 with Irish Pen and the John Hewitt Society. Her poems explore madness, stoicism, recovery and wholeness, here she turns the light on in the skeleton closet. She was diagnosed autistic aged 41.

Daniel Roy Connelly's memoir, 'Extravagant Stranger', was published by Carcanet in 2017; a poetry pamphlet, 'Donkey See, Donkey Do', was published by Eyewear in 2017; and a collection of flash fiction, 'The Incontinent of Royy', was published by Broken Sleep Books in 2022. He lives in York.

Judith Wozniak won first prize in the Hippocrates Poetry Competition, 2020. Her pamphlets, Patient Watching (2022) and Case Notes (2024) are published by Hedgehog Poetry Press. Her collection Making Dolmades in Essex by VOLE Books (2024). She has an MA in Writing Poetry from Newcastle University and The Poetry School.

Max Wallis is the author of three pamphlets and was shortlisted for the Polari Prize for his first book, Modern Love. His latest, published by Verve, is Well Done, You Didn't Die. He is the editor in chief of The Aftershock Review. His poetry has appeared in Vogue, The Rialto, Poetry London, The Spectator, and others. He was recently commended in the Magma Editors' Prize.

MAX WALLIS

Self-Portrait with Hope

if I choked no one would know
I have made my life so quiet
even an emergency would knock twice
the cats look up from their bowls
as if to say pls not now
I carry a big box of debt downstairs
almost trip and
lose my skull and even then I think well
I can't be the only one who has mistaken silence
for safety who has stood in the kitchen
holding the shape of a life like an egg
like a grenade who has wanted love
but only at a volume the nervous system
could survive outside the window
the day keeps doing its little trick
light on the bins rain on the privet
the neighbour's car door slamming me back
into my body and somewhere inside all this
my ridiculous heart with its hard hat on
walking back into the building
saying

right what now?